THE WEDDING FEAST

Margaret Doak

Illustrations by Rosemary Godfrey

Pen Press

First published in Great Britain

All paper used in the printing of this book has been made from wood grown
in managed, sustainable forests.

ISBN13: 978-1-78003-305-1

Printed and bound in the UK
Pen Press is an imprint of
Indepenpress Publishing Limited
25 Eastern Place
Brighton
BN2 1GJ

A catalogue record of this book is available from
the British Library

Cover design by Jacqueline Abromeit

For Donald, Robert and Stephen
who have taught me so much
and been with me in my spiritual
journeying.

Copyright Permissions and Acknowledgements

My thanks are due to the following publishers, copyright holders and authors for permission to use extracts and quotations from works for which they hold the copyrights, all references being noted in the text.

Cambridge University Press

1)   "Extracts from the Authorised Version of the Bible (The King James Bible) the rights in which are vested in the Crown, are reproduced by permission of the Crown's Patentee, Cambridge University Press."

2)   "Extracts from the Book of Common Prayer, the rights in which are vested in the Crown, are reproduced by permission of the Crown's Patentee, Cambridge University Press."

Continuum

3)   "Extracts from 'First to Last Adam' by C.K. Barrett (A & C Black 1962) and the poem 'Overheard in an Orchard' from 'Can she See?' by E. Cheney (Mowbrays 1996), are reproduced by kind permission of Continuum."

Eyre & Spottiswoode

4)   "Extracts from a) the Jerusalem Bible and b) Common Worship 2000 (Anglican Church) are reproduced by kind permission of Eyre & Spottiswoode, no copyright being needed."

Mimi Farra

5)   "Permission granted gratis for use of extract from 'Jesus Gave her Water', (The Holy Ghost Medley) No. 77 of 'Sounds of Living Water' (B Pulkingham, Hodder and Stoughton 1977, B Pulkingham and Jeanne Harper)."

Jeanne Harper

6)   "Permission to reproduce 'God and Man at Table are Sat Down' No. 67 from 'Sounds of Living Water' plus the penultimate verse which is reproduced by kind permission of Robert Stamps and Jeanne Harper."

Harper Collins

7)   "Extracts from the Revised Standard Version of the Bible are reprinted by permission of Harper Collins Publishers Ltd © (1946-52 & 2nd Edition of New Testament in 1971) by a Committee of Protestant and Catholic members from Great Britain, Canada and the United States (see Preface Page vi, last paragraph but one)."

Hodder and Stoughton

8)   Extracts from the New International Version of the Bible are "reproduced by permission of the publisher Hodder and Stoughton Limited", no copyright being needed, representing less than 25% of the text.

9)   In "Mans Concern with Holiness" [Edited by Marina Chavchavadze, Hodder and Stoughton, 1970] the extracts from 'The Anglican Tradition' by A.M. Allchin © is "reproduced by permission of the publisher Hodder and Stoughton Limited."

10)   Extract from "Chasing the Dragon" by Jackie Pullinger and Andrew Quicke (Hodder and Stoughton 1980) is "reproduced by permission of the publisher Hodder and Stoughton Limited."

The Lutterworth Press

11)   "For their kind permission to quote a prayer of Archbishop George Appleton from 'In His Name' (No. 203 Revised Edition 1978)."

Kevin Mayhew

12)   "For extract from 'Give me Joy in my Heart' (or 'Oil in my Lamp' according to version) from Hymns Old and New - New Anglican Edition (Traditional) arranged by Kevin Mayhew 1996. No copyright needed."

Oxford University Press

13)   "No permission is needed for use of extracts from hymns 30,131,289,299,383,407,499 in the English Hymns of 1933 being in the public domain."

S.C.M. Press

14)   "No permission is needed for a quotation from 'The Gospel According to Paul' by A.M. Hunter (S.C.M. 1962)."

CONTENTS

Note All quotations have their reference given where they occur in the text.

The Wedding Feast

Mel Tari World Mission

AN APPRECIATION

This book would never have been written without the background in which I have been privileged to live. In the order in which I have come to know them, my parents, Bishop Edmund Morgan, Archbishop George Appleton, Canon Donald Allchin, the Rev'd Robert Green, Canon Stephen Sidebotham, Canon Russ Parker who has kindly written the Foreword, to say nothing of the Rev'd David Payne and the Rev'd John Cossins and all my friends, have contributed so much to the rich web of life that is mine and which I wish to share. I am also greatly indebted to Margaret Appleton who spent many hours grappling with my script on her computer, to Rosemary Godfrey for her original drawings, to Agata Salawa Adam and her son Robert for grappling with the updating and correcting of the script and the circles, to Graham Osborn for sundry help and to Angela Legood for proof reading. Hence I have been enabled to make some attempt to tease out some of life's problems in relation to the life and work of Jesus Who invites us to become partakers with Him in His Kingdom by accepting His gift of Salvation and so share in His Wedding Feast.

Foreword by Russ Parker

Sitting down and having a meal will never be the same again if you have read this book. The Wedding Feast is an extraordinary book in which Margaret Doak illustrates how every form of enjoying food and drink becomes a window through which we can encounter Jesus and His Kingdom life and calling. She delivers a rich matrix of examples from the life of Jesus: there are parables of seed sowing and growing with invitations to feasts where some guests are dragged in and others put out because they were not ready to come to the party. There are stories of those who squandered their food like the proverbial Prodigal and the Rich Man who had plenty in the barn but no feasting in his heart. The whole of Jesus' death and resurrection are presented in the context of food: from the Last Supper meal before His execution and the eating of fish to an astonished group, who could not quite get their heads around the fact that He was risen, to the lakeside meal before His ascension and the promise of the marriage supper of the Lamb. All are proclaiming the coming of the Kingdom through the connection with feasting.

Throughout the many Bible stories which Margaret examines she weaves together threads of insight concerning spiritual hunger and the age- long human need to be welcomed, loved and healed and then empowered to serve. I suppose at the heart of all shared meals be it the simple giving of a cup of water or a four course meal is the ministry of hospitality. Father Henri Nouwen once defined hospitality as *"the space in which change is possible."* This is the core of this book. It is an invitation to rediscover our capacity to receive the hospitality of God and then to give it away to others so that they too may grow and in consequence our world comes that much closer to living the kingdom of God.

I would encourage you therefore to see reading this book as a meal in itself and that you take your time in working through the many courses on offer. There are very helpful questions and reflections at the end of each section to help you digest more thoroughly the implications of what you have found in its pages.

Every Christian has a reserved seat at the final Wedding Feast when God consummates His Kingdom amongst us. This book will help you to trace all those preparation moments in the life of Jesus and empower you to step out of the box and go and do likewise so others will also be invited.

Rev. Dr. Russ Parker

Director

Acorn Christian Healing Foundation

Feast of St. Luke the Evangelist

The Wedding Feast

Note All quotations have their reference given where they occur in the text.

III   THE DEMANDS OF THE KINGDOM I

1.   Repentance: The Prodigal Son.

2.   Humility: Instructions on going to and giving Parties.

3.   Persistence: The Friend at Midnight.

4.   Giving generously: "The Measure you give will be the Measure you get".

5.   Faith: The Lilies of the Field.

6.   Two kinds of Love: Martha and Mary.

7.   Spiritual Hunger: "Blessed are those who hunger and thirst for Righteousness".

IV   THE SECRET GROWTH OF THE KINGDOM

1.   The Sower.

2.   The Seed growing secretly.

3.   The Mustard Seed.

4.   The Lump of Leaven.

5.   The Wheat and the Weeds.

6.   The Net of Fish.

7.   Of Fig Trees, fruitful and unfruitful!

V   THE DEMANDS OF THE KINGDOM II – be prepared or else!

1.   Of Servants watching, and waiting at Table.

2.   The Rich Fool.

3.   The Rich Man (Dives) and Lazarus.

4.   The Wise and Foolish Virgins.

CONTENTS

INTRODUCTION

This book has grown out of years of pondering on the relevance for us today of what Jesus said about The Kingdom. The more I meditated, the more the Holy Spirit, Who, Jesus said, would teach us all things, (1) showed me its relevance and application. The Kingdom, as both a present and a future reality, is the true spiritual home for a Christian and so the concept is Eternal, even if the emphasis varies in different generations. Yet, as I continued to look I found that there was that same crisis element in our own generation as in Jesus' day which therefore makes all His teaching the more important for us in this topsy-turvy century of war and violence, inequality and injustice, affluence and poverty.

Over the years, too, I have been led to a particular aspect within this Kingdom teaching of Jesus, which began in the loving Father heart of God Who decreed that His Word should become Incarnate. This aspect emerged as a result of the belief that, like that Fellowship Meal which was the Last Supper and which became the great Sacrament of Holy Communion, every meal is a sacrament for Christians – a symbol of Jesus, God's Word, present with us as unseen Host. Arising from this, I was led to explore especially all those occasions in the Gospels where food or drink feature and are essential to the theme, and when Jesus was either present at dinner parties, feasts and weddings, or spoke about them. Many of them were occasions of great joy or importance and Jesus took the opportunity to drive home His teaching on the Kingdom through them. And He was on home ground here, too. The Israelites believed that they were wedded to God in their Covenant relationship with Him and that, however bad things were for them, there would come a time when God would roll down the curtain on world history and bring in His Reign of justice and peace by means of a great Banquet or Wedding Feast, (2) at which they would all be present.

Quite clearly, Jesus saw His time on earth as a foretaste of that final Wedding Feast. The Kingdom was indeed present within them (3) and His followers could begin to appropriate the blessings of the Kingdom

2

which would later reach their completion. So His presence was a time of joy, yet He pointed out that such joy could be eradicated if, once having accepted Jesus as King of the Kingdom, the radical change that was required did not bear fruit. He pointed out to the Pharisees in particular, the pious Churchmen of His day, that they could not even hope to enter the Kingdom or taste of its joys unless they were radically changed first. Since Jesus' message on the Kingdom was urgent, many aspects of His teaching were stressed and repeated, so there will be seen that same stress and recurrence in the text.

These meditations aim to show how the same situation exists for us in our day, as in each generation, and how we can apply His teachings in order to bring in the Kingdom in our own lives and in the world around us today. "The fields...are ripe for harvest." (4) The labourers are few but God's Holy Spirit will act through those channels until the harvest is complete. Then the final rejoicing can come in that Eternal Wedding Feast which is Heaven. (2)

(1)   See John 14 v 26.
(2)   See Revelation 19 v 7.
(3)   See Luke 17 v 21.
(4)   John 4 v 35.

NB: Biblical quotations are taken from the New International Version unless otherwise stated.

I   IN THE BEGINNING

A   WORD MADE FLESH

1.   OUT OF SILENCE

(Wisdom 18 vv 14-15; John 1 vv 1-5 and 14-18.)

"While all things were in quiet silence, and that night was in the midst of her swift course, thine almighty Word leaped down from heaven, out of thy royal throne" (Wisdom 18 vv 14-15). (1)

* * * * * * *

The sun has reached its midday height and the flower-beds are ablaze with colour. There is also a hum among the flowers for the bees are at work. In fact these bees have been alerted as to the whereabouts of pollen for food by a highly specialised form of communication performed in or around the beehive. A bee which has found the sweet nectar will either do a round dance suggesting that food is to be found nearby; or it will do a waggle dance, the number of waggles indicating the distance and direction of the food. Worker bees obtain this information by sensing the vibrations of the dancer. This dance will be repeated by the first bees which responded, once they have located the source of food. Then yet more bees can take up the work until there is a considerable supply of food. A social activity for the good of all, started by one dancer communicating the good news.

Have you ever thought what it would be like not to be able to communicate? Have you, seriously? The art of communication is of the essence of life. It is the ability to relate to someone else verbally, yes, but it is far more than words. There is also the whole language of our bodies – the fond look, the embrace, all the silent but meaningful visible or non-visible actions which bespeak our emotions. Without love, fellowship and companionship we perish. And how much more meaningful is a meal when taken in company, whether we communicate with words, or as a couple in love, out of the silence of the heart. It can

4

indeed be one of the most pleasurable experiences of life – and often one wishes the meal could last for ever!

If communication is necessary for our survival, both physically and emotionally, so, too, is it necessary for us spiritually. For it is God Who is the prime communicator of His Good News and without Him we die. At the beginning of time God "spake and it was done; he commanded, and it stood fast." (2) Whatever God says and wishes to accomplish is done. Both the Psalmist and the Prophet stressed that His Word *has* the authority and power to perform His every command. It never returns empty or void, (3) for God is watching over His Word to perform it. (4) Then at the right moment in time, out of the silence of Eternity, God sent His Almighty Word while "night was in the midst of her swift course" (1). That Word He allowed to become flesh – His Own Word, Incarnate, in the Person of Jesus. And He dwelt on earth for a space of time, living, working and being amongst His people in His home, at worship and at dinner parties. It was in such homely activities that Jesus, God's Word, communicated Who God is and His Love to all with whom He came into contact! So His disciples could say "And the Word was made flesh, and dwelt amongst us, (and we beheld his glory, the glory as of the only begotten of the Father,) full of grace and truth." (5) They saw Him, yes, they handled Him, and shared in every activity with Him. (6) Above all, He broke bread and drank wine in fellowship with them (7) – a foreshadowing of that Eternal Feast at the end of time. God's Word is still alive and active today, "piercing to the division of soul and spirit". (8) His Word never returns void. It performs God's every command – even winds and storms obey His Word. (9) "He sends his commands to the earth: his word runs swiftly!" (9)

We live our lives, Lord, so often forgetful of You.

Then we are brought up short by circumstances.

In that moment we turn to You and Your Word is born anew in us.

And what is that Word You speak,

That comes out of the silence of Eternity,

Enfolding us in Your Peace?

This is the Word You speak:

"Peace on earth, Goodwill to men...

How I love you My child and how I wish you loved each other." (10)

To think through:

i.   In what ways do we as humans communicate? What does this tell us about the power of communication?

ii.   What does the Bible say about God's Word ? (Look up Psalm 33 vv 6 and 9; Isaiah 55 v 11; Jeremiah 1 v 12; John 1 vv 1-14; and Hebrews 4 v 12.) What difference can be noted between God's Word and human communication?

iii.   In what ways is God's Word important to you? How can we seek to make His Word alive and active in our lives and in the world?

iv.   Do we tend to limit God Who can do abundantly more than we ask or think? If so, what do we need to do to alter this so that He can have sovereign power and authority in our lives and in the affairs of the world?

(1)   Apocrypha Authorised Version.

(2)   Psalm 33 v 9 Authorised Version.

(3)   See Isaiah 55 v 11.

(4)   See Jeremiah 1 v 12 Revised Standard Version.

(5)   John 1 v 14 Authorised Version.

(6)   See I John 1 vv 1-2.

(7)   See Luke 22 vv 14-38; I Corinthians 11 vv 23-26.

6

(8)   Hebrews 4 v 12 Revised Standard Version.

(9)   Psalm 147 v 15; see Mark 4 v 41.

(10)   Author's words based on Luke 2 v 14.

2. BETHLEHEM: HOUSE OF BREAD

(Micah 5 vv 2-4 Revised Standard Version)

"But you, O Bethlehem Ephrathah, who are little to be among the clans of Judah, from you shall come forth for me one who is to be ruler in Israel, whose origin is from of old, from ancient days... And he shall stand and feed his flock in the strength of the Lord." (vv 2 and 4)[1]

* * * * * * *

There is the famous Russian story of a man, who, as he sat at work, waited for Jesus to come as he heard Him say in a dream. He brushed aside all who came asking for help, saying he had no time for them as he was expecting an important visitor. Yet by the end of the day his visitor had not come and he went to bed disappointed. That night he had another dream in which the Lord appeared to him and asked him where he was yesterday. He replied by saying that he was waiting for Him all day, but He never came. And the Lord said that He came to visit him several times during the day but he was too busy to see Him. Yet in helping all those people who called on him he would have been helping Him. How crestfallen and ashamed the man was!

Alas, this poor man had wanted to see Jesus but he had missed the point. Being prepared to see Jesus means having our eyes open to notice the signs that God gives. The Jews had received innumerable signs. God had sent Prophet after Prophet to warn His people and to point them to the coming of the Messiah and of His Birth in Bethlehem, the home of Jesus' great ancestor, David. (1) Yes, out of Bethlehem would come One Who would rule in Israel. What could be more pointed? Yet the inhabitants of Bethlehem slept through the birth of the Saviour of the world. They were totally unprepared.

Nevertheless the Lord had prepared the hearts of at least two groups of people – the shepherds and the wise men. There were those lowly

8

__Jewish shepherds__ tending the sheep reared for sacrifice in the Temple, on the hills around Bethlehem – David himself had shepherded on these hills as a boy. (2) There the angels announced the Good News of the Saviour's birth to the shepherds who went to the manger in their simplicity. (3) Then *__Wise Men, Gentiles__* from Eastern lands, arrived after their long and arduous journey, guided by a star and bringing with them their rich and significant gifts. (4)

God had not only prepared His people, the Jews, by many signs for the coming of the Saviour but He had also prepared them for the fact that He was for all mankind, Jew and Gentile, man and woman, free born and slave. (5)

How then shall we receive the signs? Those same signs still point to the fact that the Saviour's birth was on a universal and eternal scale. His birth in Bethlehem is as pregnant with meaning for us today as it was nearly two thousand years ago. His coming *__then__* still has power for us *__now__* as we unfold the drama of His Birth through to His Death, Resurrection and Ascension and the unleashing of the Spirit at Pentecost.

Why should God bring forth His Word mysteriously through the power of the Spirit as a tiny helpless Babe and, in the eyes of the world, out of wedlock? Why should He choose Him to be born in abject poverty and in a small, little-known place, rather than in a palace? Perhaps it is because this situation speaks to some two-thirds of the world – the poor and the poorest of the poor, the downtrodden, the abused of both sexes, those made redundant, refugees and outcasts. Yes, Jesus came to call such people, people burdened by the rigours of legalism and life, and without hope. We, too, can be guided by the light of that same star to Him Who is the Light of the World. He is also the Good Shepherd (6), the Lamb of God, Who came to replace those sheep offered as ineffectual sacrifices, in a once-for-all sacrifice on the Cross. Through Him Who is the Door of the sheep, all who seek Him may go in and find Salvation. What could be more significant? Jesus, born in Bethlehem, House of Bread, was to give His body to be broken as Bread for the world and His life Blood as spiritual nourishment. (7)

Lord Jesus Christ, who in the offerings of the wise men didst receive an earnest of the worship of the nations:

Grant that thy church may never cease to proclaim the good news of thy love, that all men may come to worship thee as their Saviour and king, who livest and reignest world without end.

Come, Lord Jesus, Your Body broken as Bread for the world. Nourish us, fill us with Your joy and Your peace. (8)

To think through:

i.   Every Christmas we sing "O little Town of Bethlehem". What does Bethlehem mean for us as Christians today and for the world? Will you, like those inhabitants of Bethlehem, sleep through the present-day signs of His coming? Or will you, like the shepherds and wise men, allow yourself to hear and see God's signs as spoken in Scripture and by the Holy Spirit?

ii.   What, for us, are the signs of the Lord's coming?

iii.   In the Gospels angels communicated the Good News of Jesus' Birth. How shall we communicate the Good News of Jesus' saving Love to those who neither know nor receive Him here in Britain – to those of other faiths, or of no faith; to men and women of violence?

(1)   See I Samuel 16 v 1; see also Micah 5 vv 2-4.
(2)   See I Samuel 16 v 11; Psalm 23.
(3)   See Luke 2 v 15.
(4)   See Matthew 2 vv1-12.
(5)   See Luke 2 v 3; 3 v 6; Galatians 3 v 28.
(6)   See John 10 vv 7-20.
(7)   See John 6 vv 54-56.
(8)   A prayer of Archbishop George Appleton from "In His Name" No 203 Page 139, Lutterworth Press 1978.

3. "MAN SHALL NOT LIVE BY BREAD ALONE"

(Authorised Version)

(Matthew 4 vv 1-11. See also Luke 4 vv 1-13.)

(The devil said unto Him) "If thou be the Son of God, command that these stones be made bread." But he (Jesus) answered and said, "It is written, ' Man shall not live by bread alone, but by every word that proceedeth out of the mouth of God' " (Matthew 4 vv 3 and 4, Authorised Version).

* * * * * * *

Every year we hear of thousands of people dying by famine. We see pictures of starving people from all over Africa and other countries. We are revolted. We give money to one or other of the charities to relieve their needs and then hope to feel that our consciences are salved. We continue to eat our suppers.

Yes, and people were starving in Palestine in the time of Jesus. He already knew this when He went out into the wilderness to fast for forty days concerning His Messiahship. There, attuned to the will of God as He was through His prayer and fasting, He was nevertheless hungry after His long fast, and the devil seized his opportunity. He tempted Jesus to turn stones to bread. Jesus could easily have used His Divine power to have done so. Not only could He thus have fed Himself but also His hungry fellow countrymen. As Messiah He would in any case be expected to feed His people mysteriously, as He did later when He fed the five thousand in the wilderness, (1) re-echoing the wilderness feeding in the time of Moses. (2) Yet He did not choose the way of being a social provider.

Obviously Jesus knew that a starving man is in no position to hear the Good News if he is too weak, as is borne out in His teaching. He tells His disciples, and therefore us, to feed the hungry, (3) and to give in good measure. (4) He condemned one rich man for not caring for poor Lazarus (5) and another one for storing wheat in his barns for himself. (6) He bade his disciples share their very little food and through their doing so used the materials to feed those hungry five thousand. (1)

Throughout the ages this dilemma has presented itself. Feed people and they will be able to lift their heads and live a decent life. It is a human right.

Yes indeed, but Jesus also knew that man needs something more. "Man shall not live by bread alone, but by every word that proceedeth out of the mouth of God." He knew that the deepest need and longing, whether recognised or not, of every human being is for God Himself. So rather He would preach the Good News of the coming of God's Kingdom and give His Life, His flesh, for the salvation of each and all.

Missionaries throughout the ages have also discovered this truth afresh for themselves. They have arrived in far-flung climes to preach the Word of God before anything else. So, too, in twentieth century East Harlem, New York. Poverty-stricken people there and in such places were led to accept Christ and come into renewal of life. Once they received new life in Christ they began to reorganise their lives, build churches, clean up their lives and homes, grow crops and take stewardship seriously. And soon their bodies were being fed as well as their spirits and souls.

As I write, there is news of poverty and starvation in one part of the world or another. I am sure that, terrible as it is, God will use the time to challenge Christians to pray for the leaders of the nations and for their peoples: to pray that those who are possessed by fear, greed, evil desires and the desire to master the world will be released from such and open their hearts to receive Christ. These people are hungry, unknown to them, for God. Without Him there are many evil desires, physical and spiritual hunger, emptiness. With Him there is an infilling of the Spirit. What happened to a criminal who accepted Jesus Christ into his life can happen to anyone. He had met God. And this can be the experience of anyone who wishes it.

12

Lord, the world cries out –

"I am hungry, give me a crust of bread."

You know the needs of Your children long before.

You know they are hungry –

Hungry for Your Word.

Come, Lord, come to each one of them.

To people of all faiths or none.

Reveal Yourself to them all.

To think through:

i.   Why did Jesus reject the temptation to be a social provider?

ii.   What would you do if faced, as we are today, with the question as to whether we should feed people's hungry bodies or their hungry spirits first?

iii.   What does this temptation teach us about discipleship today?

(1)   See Matthew 14 vv 13-21; Mark 6 vv 30-44; Luke 9 vv 10-17; John 6 vv 1-15.
(2)   See Exodus 16.
(3)   See Matthew 25 vv 31-46.
(4)   See Matthew 7 v 2; Luke 6 vv 30 and 38.
(5)   See Luke 16 vv 19-31.
(6)   See Luke 12 vv 13-21.

B   DISCIPLES OF THE MESSIAH

In these next passages we shall discover from the early stories of the Gospels the exhilaration of the disciples when they met Jesus, and seek to see how that same joy can be ours today.

1.   "COME TO ME, ALL WHO LABOUR"
      (Revised Standard Version)
      (Matthew 11 vv 28 and 29.)

"Come to Me, all who labour and are heavy laden, and I will give you rest (or refreshment)" (1)
(verse 28).

* * * * * * *

I had been driving along a hot, dusty road for some time when I came to a wayside inn with a sign saying "Rest Awhile". Just what I needed. I was exhausted, having relied on my own strength to journey on, so I stopped and went in. My hosts, noticing that I looked weary, asked if I would like a bath. I gladly accepted before eating. Having washed and eaten I was rested, refreshed and restored.

Life is like this. In the Palestine of Jesus' time there were resting places along the hot, dusty roads and in the towns and villages. These little inns or khans were shake-downs for the night where you might get a wash and food, rest (or refreshment). Knowing what it was like to travel there, Jesus possibly had such resting places in mind when He said to His disciples and others who heard Him "Come to Me, all who labour and are heavy laden, and I will give you rest (or refreshment)."(1)

In some parts of the world there are still nomads who move from oasis to oasis carrying their possessions around with them, travelling as light as possible, but even so they and their animals bearing quite heavy burdens. I used to travel light before I owned a house and a car. Now I have more possessions and I push more into my car when I go on a journey, making loading and unloading burdensome!

Perhaps some of us have become wearied and weighed down with burdens which threaten to strangle our spiritual lives and separate us from others. We selfishly push others aside in our ambition to reach the top. Our pride keeps us wrapped up in cotton wool, away from the messy business of life. We travel on through life often engrossed in ourselves or throttled by our possessions until, wearied by all the effort, we begin to look for an oasis. Some have found that oasis in drugs; others have sought rest and peace through gurus, (2) yoga and transcendental meditation.

However, let us hear the words of Jesus again: "Come to me, all you who labour and are heavy laden, and I will give you rest – refreshment."(1) So let us, as we meditate, ask Jesus to release us from all that binds us, and in return receive the yoke that He makes for us. It will fit easily and comfortably with no strain. It is a yoke of gentleness and humility, of kindness and service. This yoke will give us that spiritual rest and refreshment that we are looking for. We shall be joyously set free, made new and like giants refreshed by His Spirit. We shall be washed by faith in His Blood and filled with His Heavenly food.

As we let God work in us we shall begin to enter into that Rest of which He spoke through His prophets (3) and fulfilled through Jesus. (4) This signifies not just the weekly Sabbath Rest but that Eternal Rest which belongs to life in His Kingdom and indicates the new life quickening in each of us. Jesus, the Messiah, will reign in our hearts – a foretaste of that Age to come when He will reign triumphant over the world.

Ye hear how kindly He invites;

Ye hear His words so blest –

"All ye that labour come to me,

And I will give you rest." (5)

To think through:

i.   Ponder over some of the burdens or loads that each of us carries around and that we could drop.

ii.   What do you think are the components of God's Eternal Rest/ Kingdom?

iii. How can we enter into God's Rest?

(1)   Refreshment is an equally good translation from the Greek.
(2)   Guru = spiritual teacher.
(3)   See Psalm 95 vv 8-11.
(4)   See Hebrews 4 vv 1-11.
(5)   English Hymnal 71 v 3.

2.   EARLY DISCIPLES MEET JESUS

(John 1 vv 35-51.)

"Rabbi – where are you staying?"…"Come and you will see" (vv 38-39).

* * * * * * *

I shall always remember the day when Ray received his invitation to Buckingham Palace to meet the Queen. There followed a flurry of activity in preparation – a new suit, shirt and tie, and new shoes. Then there was the extra special scrub and brush on the day and the train journey to London. Finally, the precious moment arrived when he heard the Queen say "Well done, Ray. You are a very brave man. Accept this medal in honour of your service to our country." Ray beamed, shook hands and bowed. The moment was over but Ray was always to treasure it..

It must have been very much the same thrill for Andrew and John when Jesus, the Messiah, came and stood where John the Baptist was preaching. At once he recognised Jesus as the Messiah for Whom he had been urging people to repent. "Behold, the Lamb of God." (1) John's witness to Jesus was electrifying. Andrew and John, already disciples of the Baptist, were more than a little curious, especially as they must have witnessed the Baptism of Jesus (see VII, 2). They wanted to know more about Jesus, so they asked Him where He was staying. As with Ray, here was their most joyful moment when they received the Invitation, "Come and you will see." (1)

The Divine Invitation was taken up and accepted. As it was late afternoon they stayed the remainder of that day with Jesus. Again, like Ray, they were never to forget their time with Him. But their encounter touched them so deeply that they wanted to continue to be with Him and be in the vanguard of His entourage. So they left John the Baptist and all their pre-conceived ideas behind. At the same time they could not wait to share their joy of the Good News that they had discovered and very soon disciples were added unto the Lord. For Andrew gained the heart of a missionary – and he fairly rushed to fetch his brother, impetuous Simon, to Jesus, Who renamed him Peter, the rock-man. (2) Jesus then met Philip (a friend of Andrew and Peter) who introduced Nathanael to Him. Nathanael discovered that Jesus could penetrate men's hearts and now in this new era required and blessed people who were pure like himself. So, too, they could exclaim that Jesus was "The Messiah", "The Son of God." (3) Jesus promised that they would see a greater revelation than ever cunning Jacob saw, through His Crucifixion, Resurrection and Ascension, when dynamic new life would break forth from the tomb, later to be liberated for all by His Holy Spirit. Through the transfiguring experience of being with the Messiah they would see "Heaven open" (3) and many would be touched by the fact that they had been with Jesus and so become disciples, too.

Jesus invites each one of us to "come and see." What is your response to such an Invitation?

Invitation

Lord, it is indeed wonderful to receive an Invitation from You.

We are so unworthy, yet You seek us out.

And when we have met You, life can never be the same again.

Grant, dear Lord, that we may not tarnish that new life;

And that others may see Your Light, recognise Your Glory

shining out

And so themselves be drawn to You.

To think through:

i.   Discuss what pre-conceived ideas Christians and others have about Christ. Do we need to discard any of them?

ii.   Are we prepared to stake our all and proclaim the Good News of Jesus with the same fervour as Andrew and Philip? If so, how will we do it?

iii.   What does purity of heart mean?

iv.   Do we take people to church or to Jesus? What is the difference?

(1)   John 1 v 29 Authorised Version.
(2)   See also Matthew 16 v 18.
(3)   John 1 vv 41, 49, 51.

3.   THE WEDDING FEAST AT CANA

(John 2 vv 1-11.)

Jesus said to the servants "Fill the jars with water". So they filled them to the brim (verse 7).

* * * * * * *

Most people love going to weddings for the joy and promise of future happiness they bring. Jesus enjoyed them, too. In the Old Testament, weddings and wedding feasts symbolised God's generosity and goodness and His binding Covenant relationship with the Jews. They were also seen as a foretaste of the future delights of the presence of the Messiah when God and His people would be united forever in a new, unbroken relationship of fidelity.

Here is a wedding full of the joys of the occasion. The whole village would have dropped in at some time during the week of festivities. Yet I'm sure that many others also turned up out of curiosity because the news had spread that Jesus and His disciples (most of whom came from Galilee) had been invited. People would almost certainly be hoping that He would perform some miraculous sign to show that He was the long-awaited Messiah.

For the discerning this wedding was pregnant with Divine Love and Grace breaking through and Jesus' very presence was a sign of this in itself. His action of changing water into wine – and in such a vast quantity – was also a symbol of that superabundance which is God's alone to give. Here certainly, was a couple in need and a word changed a humiliating situation into one of joy. And that same Word was vibrant with the Divine Power of the Creator. God has always rejoiced over His Creation, (1) despite human sin, and the presence of the Messiah at this wedding was of special significance for Judaism. His disciples came to see His action as transcending the dull, arid and stifling pettiness of the Law. God was showing that He was less concerned about the rites of outer purification than about the exhilarating transformation that would take place in people when they tasted the sparkling new wine of the New Covenant. Later this New Covenant would be sealed and cemented by the loving sacrifice of the Blood of the Lamb – a foreshadowing of the Eucharistic rite. Judaism had become ossified and was now being superseded. From now on, the Kingdom to which they had looked forward was within, or among, them. (2) His disciples recognised this, though His Glory and the nature of the Kingdom remained veiled until later.

Jesus' Spirit is still present in our midst two thousand years on – even if still unrecognised by so many. Alas, there is much to grieve His heart, but He is the same today as yesterday, (3) and He continues to be in love with His world and His people. He forever pours out His Spirit to overflowing. Indeed we have seen a wonderful outpouring of grace to many individuals and churches in our own time, both here in Britain and in Northern Ireland, where Catholics and Protestants are working together to bring reconciliation through God's Spirit in a still tenuously-held peace there. So, too, in the Arab world and Africa, to name but a few. Africa has one of the fastest growing Churches in the world. When I asked one joyful-looking African Bishop to what he attributed such spiritual growth, he replied "We pray and we pray and we pray – and prayer includes praise." The Lord does not need us to pray for Him to know that we want His Holy Spirit and His good gifts but our prayer and praise shows our desire to bring forth the request. It would seem that the couple at Cana did not ask. Rather Mary did. Yes, God does give His Spirit freely, yet the fullness of that out-pouring can only come to full fruition when we desire it and long to appropriate it. Wherever there has been an outpouring of the Holy Spirit it has been preceded with much prayer, as many Jews had done throughout the ages. (4) Then others reap the benefits.

Within our own situations we need to ask for and long for God's Reign to break through in our lives – even perhaps more fully, to sanctify and bless our marriages, our families, our friendships and work relationships, and the everyday tasks and events of our lives. Every activity, every meal is a sacrament – a sign of God's presence with us.

Lord, we ask You to grace our lives with Your presence,

Just as You graced the Wedding Feast at Cana.

Without You our lives are dried up.

Without You we lose that cutting edge.

Filled with Your Spirit, may we become as new wine,

Bubbling up, our spirits filled to overflowing.

So we pray that we may be channels

By which others may know You and Your reign.

To think through:

i.   What symbolism did you notice in the story of the Wedding Feast?

ii. What signs do you see of God's workings in your church? Thank God for any you see and pray for Him to increase His work of grace further.

iii. What does this story tell us about the Love and power of God and
the Reign of the Messiah?

(1)   See Genesis 1 v 31.
(2)   See Luke 17 v 21.
(3)   See Hebrews 13 v 8.
(4)   See Luke 2 vv 25f and 36f.

4.   THE MIRACULOUS DRAUGHT OF FISH

(Luke 5 vv 1-11. See also Mark 1 vv 16-20; Matthew 4 vv 18-22;

John 1 vv 35-42.)

"Put out into deep water, and let down the nets for a catch"... "Don't be afraid; from now on you will be catching men" (vv 4 and 10).

* * * * * * *

The sun, shining over the Sea of Galilee, must have sparkled more brightly where Jesus sat in Simon Peter's boat preaching to the crowds on the shore. Then, suddenly, He had finished and He was telling Peter to launch his nets out into the deep for a catch. Now Simon Peter was a master fisherman but here was Someone Who, albeit the Messiah, was no fisherman, but rather a Carpenter telling him what to do! Had he not toiled fruitlessly all night in the cold? Yet there was that compelling note of authority again, so he replied: "Master...because you say so, I will" (1) even though it was by this time broad daylight! The catch was effortless, yet so large that their nets began to break. So he and Andrew called for their partners, James and John, to help.

Such an encounter brought Simon Peter to his knees. All his ideas of himself as a person, as a master fisherman, vanished. He recognised his unworthiness before the Man Whom he was to acknowledge as Lord of All. Jesus had wanted to burn into these men's hearts and minds that, because they had obeyed, even before they had that deeper faith, He could use them for bringing people into God's Kingdom. And so it was that these four men left all that very day – their families and fishing – and followed Jesus.

Are we ministers of the Word, ordained or lay, even ordinary Christians, fervent in sharing our faith, trying to win souls to God? We love the Lord and yet, somehow, the numbers just do not increase. There is apathy and indifference all around affecting even our own lives. Have we become unintentionally immersed in more earthly pursuits and the fire which fanned our first love for the Lord been all but extinguished? We are saddened. Why is St Agatha's down the road so full or in a more advantageous position when St Blasius here is half-empty? The answer lies in ourselves. We may have been fervently running around for God, yet we have not allowed Him to have His way in our lives.

So let us hear anew His Word for us, spoken gently, yet with authority. But we shall have to **_want_** this, for one of the reasons why we toil so fruitlessly is that we have been jealously guarding the church and its traditions at St Maud's for ourselves and criticising our fellow Christians who think differently, thus actually preventing souls from coming into the net. We will have to relinquish all our own importance, all that we hold dear and our own vain efforts. Why not let down all the shutters and just relax, fill ourselves afresh with His Love and His Word and allow Him to fill us with His Life-giving Spirit? He will bathe and anoint us with His power.

Under His direction, then, God can begin to use us as channels of His Love and grace. If, in obedience, even when faith seems difficult, we "launch" our nets "out into the deep", (1) the flood-gates really will open. Then there will be so many coming into the Kingdom that the "seams" of the church buildings will begin to burst. Existing structures may have to come down to accommodate, but assuredly there will be a mighty harvest of souls.

Lord, You have asked me to let down the nets – launch out into the deep.

It's difficult Lord, I can't see the way ahead.

But wait; yes, I hear Your gentle, calm voice speaking with authority.

And I know that I can trust You as I take Your hand.

You have shown me sufficient to take the next step.

Lord, I praise You and I recognise my own littleness in Your sight.

I realise that this way means that You are in control – not I.

This way means that Your plans are Sovereign, not mine.

All my petty plans, my preconceived ideas, all my earthly whims

Which prevent others from knowing You, simply melt in Your light.

This way means that Your Glory is revealed,

And people seeing it will be caught up into the Kingdom.

To think through:

i.   Think about what it means to launch out into the deep for us today. What difficulties present themselves

        (a)   to us as individuals

        (b)   to the Church as a whole or locally?

ii.   What are some of the dearly held traditions that prevent us from launching out into the deep? What Tradition should we keep and why? (See also II 3.)

iii.   Why is it that one church seems to be going ahead whilst another is dying on its feet? What might be some of the causes? Do we see any signs of decadence or growth in our own church and if so, how can we improve on or further the situation?

(1)   Luke5 v 5.

II   THE OLD ORDER CHANGETH: OR THE NEW DISPENSATION

INTRODUCTION

During this week we shall see how, once the Kingdom is established in our lives, Jesus challenges us to change our old ways and traditions for His ways.

1.   PLUCKING EARS OF CORN

(Matthew 12 vv 1-8; Mark 2 vv 23-28; Luke 6 vv 1-5.)

"The Sabbath was made for man, not man for the Sabbath" (Mark 2 v 27).

* * * * * * *

It was one of those golden summer days when it would soon be harvest. Maybe we have strolled through a cornfield like Jesus' disciples, picking and rubbing ears of corn. Jewish Law allowed hungry travellers to do this, (1) but not on the Sabbath (2) because it was considered to be a primitive form of threshing.

When the Pharisees criticised Jesus for allowing His disciples to do this on the Sabbath He reminded them how David and his men, when hungry, ate the Bread dedicated to God – even lied to get it. (3) Yet their miscreant hero had remained uncondemned! They were even inconsistent in their own practice of the Sabbath, for the priests of the Temple were actually obliged to offer double sacrifices then! (4)

In creating the world God had made even the Sabbath subject to His unchangeable Laws and ceaseless activity of creating and sustaining the world, of mercy and of justice (judgment). And Jesus, the "Son of Man", was also Creator and Lord of the Sabbath. So He declared that His disciples had the right to enjoy God on this day in worship, in recreation, in feasting and in all the spiritual delights of that Sabbath Rest of the dawning Messianic Age, which had already been foretold. (5) By His action Jesus unshackled the Sabbath from the bondage of the Law and the hypocrisy of the Pharisees, leaving it free for true worship, the outward expression of which was to show love and mercy to their neighbours. (6)

It is good that we have moved away from the over-strict view of 'the Sabbath' in the nineteenth century, but should games be played professionally or all the shops opened on a Sunday today? Although most people involved might not go to church anyway, nevertheless is it not good in this age of stress and burn-out to cease as far as possible from our restless activity to refresh our bodies, minds and spirits, and our family life, for at least one day a week?

The important factor for Christians, however, will be that if the Lord is Sovereign in our lives then we will want whatever we do on Sundays to be to His Glory. Jesus Himself went to worship in the synagogue on the Sabbath and if He saw anyone in need He would heal that person right there in the synagogue or anywhere else, showing God's Love and mercy to people on the day that He Himself had created. (7) So here is a yard-stick for us – worship and fellowship (unless one has to work on a Sunday for the good of all), refreshment and re-creation, and works of mercy. This may well mean visiting sick relatives and friends, those in prison, or even providing lunch for the homeless. Or it might mean inviting the neighbour sitting there without heat or friends, the lonely, the single or the widowed.

Whatever we do to enhance God's Glory, even if it means breaking our hide-bound rules or precious traditions, it will give us the joy of sharing His Love and of entering into that Sabbath Day's Rest that belongs to the Kingdom.

Lord, grant that we may treat Your Holy Day with respect,

That we may seek Your face and fellowship,

Yet at the same time show Your Love and mercy

To all Your family and friends.

To think through:

i. What does Jesus mean by saying "The Sabbath was made for man, not man for the Sabbath" (Mark 2 v 27)?

ii. Which do you think has priority: to go to church on Sunday or to hold the hand of someone dying? Also, do we jealously guard Sunday for ourselves and our families, or do we share the day with others? Indeed do we know where the lonely, the sick, the single and widowed near us are?

iii. It is a good thing that we have moved away from the over-strict view of the 'Sabbath' as in the nineteenth century but should Christians partake in professional games, go shopping or do household jobs on a Sunday? Should they not set a different example? What reasons can you give for and against such events on a Sunday for Christians?

(1)   See Deuteronomy 23 v 25.
(2)   See Exodus 20 vv 8-11.
(3)   See I Samuel 21 vv 1-7.
(4)   See Numbers 28 vv 9-10.
(5)   See Isaiah 25 vv 6-9.
(6)   See Hosea 6 v 6; Matthew 12 v 7.
(7)   See Luke 13 vv 10-17; 14 vv 1-6.

2.   JESUS EATS WITH LEVI, TAX COLLECTORS AND SINNERS

(Matthew 9 vv 9-13; Mark 2 vv 13-17; Luke 5 vv 27-32.)

"Those who are well have no need of a physician, but those who are sick. Go and learn what this means, 'I desire mercy, and not sacrifice'. For I came not to call the righteous, but sinners" ("to repentance" – Luke) (Matthew 9 vv 12-13) (Revised Standard Version).

* * * * * * *

Jesus had obviously noticed what sort of person Levi, or Matthew, was, or He could make of him. Matthew, too, may well have noticed Jesus working in and around the busy cosmopolitan lakeside port of Capernaum, in the Synagogue and in private homes like Peter's. However, whether he knew much about Him or not, Jesus' call had that note of authority which made Matthew get up instantly, leave his tax office by the seashore for ever and follow Him.

Matthew was so grateful to Jesus and so thrilled that he gathered together all his friends – other tax collectors and sinners (1) – and made a great feast for Him so that they could meet Him. The Pharisees learned of it and accused Jesus to His disciples of eating and drinking with disreputable people (1) – hardly the thing for a devout Jewish Teacher, they thought! (2) However, Jesus was often at such dinner parties precisely so that He could be with those whom He had come to help and save... Yes, this was the burden of Jesus' message. He came to save the sick and disreputable people of society...

How then shall we receive this message? We, too, have created our sects in society – those who 'go to church', and those who do not go or are drop-outs; those who have accepted Jesus as Saviour and Lord and who follow His commands, and those who have not – a 'them' and 'us' situation. Alas, how often do we, who go to church, or say that we are Christians, actually prevent those who do not go to church from going, or from committing themselves to Christ? How many of us have shut ourselves off in a clique, not prayed for the vicar or members of the congregation, whether we agree with them or not, or sided with one group against another? How often has our church-going just stopped there? Or do we need it said to us "I desire mercy and not sacrifice" (3) – love, kindness and generosity to those who think differently from us and those whose behaviour society frowns upon? Unless we change we may find the unrighteous and the lost attending the Wedding before us. (4)

So we may find ourselves with a host of different friends – ex-prisoners, drug addicts or alcoholics – the lost of society whom Jesus came to save and account as righteous. Can we face it? Those early disciples did. I have seen many, including criminals and prisoners, changed by the Living Christ, filled with the Spirit and then used by the Lord to bring others into the Kingdom. We have to ask ourselves first, though, do we want to see those whom society despises in the Kingdom, filling our churches? If so, fine…

We are sitting, waiting in our little tax office when we receive a call from Jesus. Are we ready, like Matthew, to rise up and follow, to honour the Lord with a dinner party…? But first, let us like Zacchaeus (5) present Him with our own earthly 'treasures' – all those things in our lives that we want to hold on to – position, honour, wealth, our own goodness, even our pride and snobbishness. And in their place let us invite to the feast those whom in the past we may have left outside.

Lord, when I look at myself and the world

I realise that there is not one righteous, save by Your Grace.

Without You, we are sick, lost, unwholesome.

Let us, like Matthew, hasten to rise up and accept Your call.

All our costliest treasures we now offer to You, dear Lord,

And in their place we come to receive Your Blessings.

To think through:

i.   How, and in what ways, might Christians be said to prevent those who are not Christians from committing themselves to Christ?

ii.   How do we show love and mercy in our lives? What could be done to improve on it? Does it include involving ourselves in a more 'grass roots' way with the "lost of society"? If so, how? And who are the lost? (NB Not just the obvious ones.)

iii.   What does God's Righteousness consist of?

(1)   Sinners were those who failed even to attempt to keep the vast body of Jewish Law and would not normally attend the synagogue for worship.
(2)   See Matthew 11 vv 18-19; Luke 7 vv 33-35.
(3)   Hosea 6 v 6; Matthew 9 v 13.
(4)   See Matthew 21 vv 31-32.
(5)   See Luke 19 v 8.

3. TWO VIEWS OF THE LAW

(Mark 7 vv 1-23; Matthew 15 vv 1-20. See also Luke 11 vv 37-44.)

"Nothing that goes into a man from outside can make him unclean; it is the things that come out of a man that make him unclean" (Mark 7 v 15, Jerusalem Bible).

* * * * * * *

Among the Aboriginals of Australia or the head-hunting tribes of Papua New Guinea one might still find whole communities regulated and ruled by tradition. Most of this appertains to ceremonies and rituals – such as the ceremony used to instal a new chieftain, or how to conduct rites of initiation for teenage youths. Such tradition has been handed down orally by the elders of the tribes. Yet at the same time tradition is different from the sacred Law of the tribe which governs its daily life.

So, too, the Jews in the time of Jesus. Tradition concerning Ceremony and Ritual had been handed down from Rabbi to Rabbi over and above the sacred Law – The Ten Commandments (1) and Ethical Codes. Over the years their Tradition had been added to and not only had become a heavy burden for people to bear but also much of it was petty and meaningless. And some of the Tradition even seemed to supersede the Ten Commandments and moral teaching of Prophets like Amos, Isaiah and Hosea about love, mercy and justice, as Jesus pointed out to them (2).

The Pharisees were shocked when Jesus suggested that they were not clean morally even through their ritual washings; moreover they were not honouring their parents as the Fifth Commandment stated they should, despite giving their dues to God. And they were not keeping His Holy Laws of justice and love, despite tithing. Only by keeping the Ten Commandments, to which they were not too attached, rather than Tradition, by purifying their hearts, and therefore their actions, and by giving to the poor in love and justice could they be said to be showing true religion!

We, too, have our tradition with its ceremonies and rituals which have become encrusted and meaningless, even taking precedence over God's Laws. It does not take long to discover that Christianity itself is often deeply immersed in tradition and can even impede and distract Christians from keeping them. Issues such as holding on to the Book of Common Prayer, (3) certain rituals and ceremonies in worship, or discussions on Ministry today have nothing to do with the keeping of God's Holy Laws and much time and energy is wasted on them. Society, including many Christians, seems to condone the breaking of every single Commandment and even the laws of our country, flagrantly disregarding both those concerning God and those concerning one's neighbour, or fellow humans of whatever class, race or creed. Tradition furthermore often keeps us in tight-knit compartments which prevent us from helping our neighbour.

It is easier to uphold tradition rather than the Law, for tradition protects and shields us from the change that would destroy us. Tradition is also less disturbing, for it does not make the same demands as the Law, yet it shows the world our attachment to religion, however slight. There is, however, a Tradition that we should keep – Jesus' command to love one another and to receive His Body and Blood in remembrance of – or calling to mind – His Presence. (See VII 6.)

However, God's Holy Spirit is at work despite the current laxity and evils. Tradition has been knocked on the head in some areas. In Northern Ireland the tradition and hatred which separated so many has also counter-produced some startling results where God's Laws of Love and justice are joyfully proclaimed in a variety of communities including Catholic and Protestant alike. And some of our churches have overthrown tradition to work together on issues such as poverty and justice both at home and abroad in the Third and Fourth worlds, aiming to bring the Good News to God's people in such places.

Even so, this is only the tip of the iceberg. We still need to allow God's Holy Spirit to stir us on to further action.

36

Lord help us to see that our man-made tradition binds us and that we cannot be satisfied with anything less than the keeping of Your Laws. That Law, the Law of love, is the only one, for if Your Love is the mainspring of our hearts we shall want to see our neighbours treated fairly and justly.

To think through:

i.   What sacrifices would we need to make in order that Christ's Church may grow? Are we willing to make these?

ii.   Where in the Church, either here or elsewhere in the world, do we see signs of God's Holy Spirit at work and in what ways?

iii. What does Jesus mean when He says "What comes out of a man is what makes him unclean"? (4) What do you think God's Holy Laws for Christians are?

(1)   See Exodus 20.

(2)   See Matthew 12 v 7; also Amos 5 v 24; Psalm 85 v 10.

(3)   The 1662 Prayer Book of the Church of England.

(4)   Mark 7 v 20.

4.   TO FAST OR NOT TO FAST!

(Mark 2 vv 18-20; Matthew 9 vv 14-15; Luke 5 vv 33-35.)

"How can the guests of the bridegroom fast while he is with them?…
The time will come when the bridegroom will be taken from them, and
on that day they will fast" (Mark 2 vv 19-20).

* * * * * * *

I remember that first time when I went away without my dog. He was
apparently dispirited whilst I was away but when I returned home he
was so overjoyed that I just had to sit on the floor so that he could
frolic about me in celebration of my return.

In response to the question about fasting Jesus is quite clearly saying
that there is a time to fast and a time **_not_** to fast. His presence on earth
was one such occasion, for God was visiting and redeeming His people.
Quintessentially it was a time for joy. In this delightful conversation
Jesus clearly equates Himself with the Bridegroom – the Messiah –
and His disciples with the wedding guests or attendants. Here was a
foretaste of that great Wedding Feast of the end of the Age.

Jesus continues to be present with those who seek Him and He fills
them with that same joy – a deep inner joy that the world cannot take
away. We see this joy in the life of a Saint Francis, or a twentieth
century martyr like Mother Maria Skobtsova, who allowed herself to
die in place of another in the gas chamber at the end of the Second
World War for that deep inner joy that was hers as a disciple of Jesus.

Mother Maria, however, knew also what it was to fast, for she would
often give away her own very meagre rations. And Jesus knew
what it was to fast before her. He fasted for forty days and nights
in the wilderness before He began His ministry. (1) He often went
out before dawn and before breakfast to pray, and perhaps fast, in a
lonely place. (2) Clearly, too, He saw the necessity to fast before some

important event or crisis so that His physical, mental and spiritual powers were more sharply awakened and attuned for communion with His Father. This seems to have been the case with "The Boy with an Evil Spirit" as indicated in most versions, either in the text or in a footnote. (3)

Since Jesus Himself saw the necessity of fasting, then naturally He would recommend it for much the same reasons for His followers, at least from when He would be taken from them. Then "on that day they will fast" out of love, reverence and sorrow for what had happened as well as in the face of some important event or crisis.

Jesus also had words to say about fasting which are as relevant for us now as they were for His first disciples, despite a less rigid approach (its almost non-existence) in our churches today. He believed it had its place as a discipline. (4) And further He saw it as a means to a relationship of loving trust and dependence upon God. Fasting was to be a secret between the two, undertaken by a believer with a cheerful countenance, (5) the outer expression of an inner joy. Fasting brings us closer to God so that we may seek Him, learn His Will, and lay before Him in sorrow and mourning our own sin and that of the world, especially when that sin means that two-thirds of the world are starving.

The concept of fasting is taken a stage further when Jesus emphasised obeying the spirit of the Ten Commandments, and refraining from the baser passions of our sinful nature (6) to gratify our physical greed and sexual desires. Greed covers a multitude of sins, from over-eating and acquisition of material possessions to desire for power, money and influence. Sexual desires in this century include pornography and a whole range of sins connected with the senses, overtly sexual and otherwise.

For Christians down the ages fasting is in effect the renunciation of a certain life-style – that of the world – and involves a redirection of time, energy, money, talents and abilities in joyful service of the Lord.

Dear Lord, I see now that fasting is an outward expression of my love for You and the joy that springs from that relationship, so attuning my spirit with Yours. So You ask me to refrain joyfully from evil, and from food from time to time, to recall what we have done to You – crucified You! – and to share what we have spiritually, materially and physically with others.

To think through:

i.   Why did Jesus see fasting as important (a) for Himself, (b) for His disciples? What are some of the spiritual reasons for, and results of, fasting and how can we incorporate this into our life-style in the twenty-first century?

ii. How do the Ten Commandments reflect a spirit of discipline akin to fasting?

iii. Are the Ten Commandments still an essential element of Christian life today?

iv. How can one avoid fasting becoming a mere ritual or an aid to slimming?

(1)   See Matthew 4 v 2; Luke 4 v 2.

(2)   See Mark 1 v 35.

(3)   See Matthew 17 vv 14-20; Mark 9 vv 14-28; (Luke 9 vv 37-45).

(4)   See Matthew 6 vv 16-18.

(5)   Ibid.

(6)   See Mark 7 vv 20-23.

40

5.   NEW WINE IN NEW WINE SKINS!

(Mark 2 vv 21-22; Matthew 9 vv 16-17; Luke 5 vv 36-39.)

"No-one sews a patch of unshrunk cloth on an old garment… And no-one pours new wine into old wine-skins" (Mark 2 vv 21-22).

* * * * * * *

We are so familiar with our words 'old' and 'new' that their vitality and dynamism have become lost in English. 'Old' should suggest something gone, passed away, worn out. And 'new' should suggest something fresh and vital. So we take another look at these words. The Greek 'Η *KAINH* ΔIAΘHKH – HE *KAINE* DIATHEKE' – The NEW Covenant, or promise, in English suggests that the old one has passed away and a new, vital one has taken its place.

Into this world, worn out by legalism and sin, came Jesus, applying new cloth, so strong that it would tear the old cloth; and new wine, so powerful that it would burst the brittle old leather wine-skins. Both the new cloth and the new wine are like dynamite (1) blasting away the old. And Jesus came to blast away the old in order to make a NEW CREATION. "If anyone is in Christ, he is a new creation: the old has gone, the new has come." (2) Paul saw that Jesus was recreating the world by recreating individuals within it who would joyfully spread the Good News. We have to cleanse out the "old yeast" (of malice) so that we "may be a new batch without yeast". (3) Our old self has to be crucified with Him by being baptised into the Death of Christ, so that we might walk in newness of life. (4)

Maybe right now we need the power of the Holy Spirit to blast (clear) away some of the accumulated rubbish and débris in our lives and to revivify us. We fill our lives with so many things to do – church, good works, hobbies – yet with no central point holding them together and no time left for quiet reflection in the presence of the Lord. We may have a rule of life which has become heavily over-burdened. Perhaps we get up early to pray, even earnestly, but the very prayers have no life, no love in them. The Spirit is not present and so our relationship with God is lifeless. We need to turn to Him in repentance, seeking His forgiveness and then ask Him to pour down the fire of His Holy Spirit to fill us with His Love so that we may share it with others. And if we ask, we must expect to receive. Luke warns us that some people actually prefer the old, for it is more comfortable.(5) True, we must not seek change just for the sake of change, but do so if the old is worn out or no longer speaks to us. So, too, our church services. Do they still speak to both young and old, or do they, too, need the quickening fire of the Holy Spirit – not just a change in style of worship? Jesus promised His disciples Power from on High, (6) and when they received the Holy Spirit's Power on the Day of Pentecost they were as new men who were accused of being drunk. BUT they converted three thousand souls to Christ on that very day. (7) Make no mistake. He is full of power – dynamite. There is no compromise. We cannot live the life of the Spirit and the old life.

Exercise:

Read Romans 8 vv 1-17 and ask the Lord to cleanse you and fill you with new wine so that you may be an effective channel of God's Love for a world awaiting renewal.

Lord, how wonderful that You help us to exchange old lives for new.

So often we find that our lives have become frayed round the edges -

Ragged from over-burdening ourselves.

Help us, Lord, to slow down for a time -

To rid ourselves of all that hinders our effectiveness as disciples,

Allow ourselves to be filled with Your Holy Spirit – NEW LIFE.

Then we shall be able to go out as channels of Your Love,

Achieving more for Your Kingdom through Your power in us.

To think through:

i.   What do the four following readings tell us happens to the person
      who is "in Christ"?
      Romans 5 v 17.
      I Corinthians 5 vv 7-8.
      II Corinthians 5 v 17.
      Colossians 2 v 12.

ii.   What do we need for all that is old and encrusted in our lives to
      disappear and to allow the new wine of Christ to take over? What
      would we like to see "blasted away" (a) in our own lives and (b)
      in the life of the Church?

iii. How can we become effective channels of God's grace to a world
      awaiting renewal? Read Romans 8 vv 1-27.

      (1) Dunamos in Greek = Power. See Mark 1 vv 21-28.
      (2) II Corinthians 5 v 17.
      (3) I Corinthians 5 vv 7-8.
      (4) See Romans 6 vv 3-4; Colossians 2 v 12.
      (5) See Luke 5 v 39.
      (6) See Acts 1 v 8.
      (7) See Acts 2 vv 13 and 41.

6.   JESUS MEETS A WOMAN AT JACOB'S WELL

(John 4 vv 1-42.)

"Whoever drinks the water I give him will never thirst. Indeed the water I give him will become in him a spring of water welling up to eternal life" (Verse 14).

* * * * * * *

What a priceless story this is! Here we see a very human Jesus, hungry, thirsty and weary, waiting for His disciples. Yet we also see a Power at work that is more than human. Here, too, we see a woman who came on her own to draw water in the heat of the day! "Will you give me a drink?" asked Jesus, sitting by the well of their common ancestor, Jacob. The woman must indeed have wondered. A Man talking to a woman! A Jew, talking to a Samaritan! (1) And then He offered her water welling up to Eternal Life. (From 727 BC the Jews of the North Kingdom had become a mixed race resulting from foreign invasion. Antagonism had arisen between the people of the North, who became Samaritans, and those of the South, the Jews, and this lasted on into Jesus' time.)

Jesus entered into the very depths of that woman's life, gradually drawing her to Himself and gently prising out of her what was wrong with her life. "I have no husband" she said. Jesus replied "you have had five…" (v 17)The woman was amazed but not annoyed to hear about her lifestyle and finally she accepted that she had met the Messiah.

In that conversation Jesus broke down all the personal, social, racial and religious barriers that existed between herself and God, caused by sin. This is a symbolic story and a parable of Jesus' Life and Death, for He came to free us from the trammels of sin that keep us apart from God and one another. All too often we live with our fears and guilt, which we rationalise, and then, even unwittingly, we ostracise those who are different from us. Alas that we think we are 'religious' if we perform all kinds of religious duties or know all the theological stand-points. So we need freeing from, and forgiving for, all that separates us from God.

Indeed Jesus challenges us to an encounter with Him that will change us. Instead of the still, stale waters of our present lives Jesus offers us the gift of Kingdom life-the Living Water of His liberating Spirit (2) so that we may drink deeply, be cleansed and filled to overflowing in a totally new, living and dynamic relationship with Him Who is our Saviour.

This Jesus is also Saviour of the World. Our twenty-first century world needs Christ more than ever. We, too, have our personal, social, racial and religious barriers. Social and economic rifts exist between the Third and Fourth Worlds and the affluent societies, and even here in Britain between rich and poor, north and south. It is a long haul before all races can mix freely. Apartheid still exists, whether openly or in a more disguised, subtle way. Christians are still divided from one another much as Jews and Samaritans were. Evil still has free play in our lives and in the world.

The Good News, however, is still available today. Jesus has overcome evil on the Cross and through His Holy Spirit every single person can overcome it, too. He sets individuals free – you and me – like that Samaritan woman, then He bids us to go and share His Good News with family and friends and finally to 'reach out to the world' where souls are yearning for deliverance. "The fields... are white already to harvest." (3) The presence of the Holy Spirit in our midst this century has a note of urgency about the harvesting and we are God's hands, feet and voice. (4)

When the harvesting of souls is complete we will receive our wages, that is, Eternal Life in its fulness in the Kingdom.

Jesus gave her water that was not from the well,

Gave her living water and sent her forth to tell:

She went away singing, and came back bringing

Others for the water that was not from the well. (5)

To think through:

i.   What unusual features are present in the opening verses of this story?

ii.   What barriers did Jesus break down in His interview with the Samaritan woman? How are the same barriers broken down for us in Christ and in what ways does encounter with Jesus challenge and change us?

iii. For whom does Jesus say the Good News is intended and who is to take the message?

iv.   How will we reach out to those around us and the rest of the world?

(1)   There were strict social conventions in force for each group.
(2)   See also John 7 vv 37-39.II 7.
(3)   John 4 v 35 Authorised Version.
(4)   See Luke 10 v 2.
(5)   From *The Holy Ghost Medley*. Sounds of Living Water 77. By B. Pulkingham and J. Harper (Hodder & Stoughton 1977).

7.   JESUS' OFFER OF WATER AT THE FEAST OF

TABERNACLES

(John 7 vv 37-39. See also Isaiah 55 vv 1-3; Ezekiel 47 vv 1-12; and

Zechariah 14 vv 8-9.)

"If anyone is thirsty, let him come to me and drink. Whoever believes in me, as the Scripture has said, 'Streams of living water will flow from within him' " (John 7 vv 37-38). (1)

* * * * * * *

If you have ever seen water ballet you will know the exuberant feeling as "coloured" waters intermingle, dancing, sparkling and shooting up ever higher and criss-crossing to the music. It must have been like this at the Feast of Tabernacles. This was a richly symbolic and joyful thanksgiving for the grape harvest, enjoyed by the whole family, who camped out for eight days and nights to remind them of how their ancestors dwelt in tents in the wilderness. (2) On the eighth day all those present in Jerusalem would gather in the Temple courtyard for the ceremony of Drawing the Water. Water would be brought in a golden flagon from the nearby pool of Siloam in procession as an offering to God, Who, they believed and prayed, would accept their offering of what was His, and in response would replenish the parched earth.

Jesus' offer of the fresh, Living Water of the New Dispensation at the end of this ceremony fused, fulfilled and transcended Prophetic and Rabbinic Teaching in a new and exciting way. God's precious call to the Jews of old: "Come, all you who are thirsty" (3) and His promise to "pour water on the thirsty land"(4) and His Spirit upon their descendants (4) was about to happen. "Streams of living water will flow from within" the person who believes in Jesus.

Yes, "If anyone is thirsty, let him come to me and drink", cried Jesus. And for those who actually met Him this was the promise of a radical change within them, as with Peter, Mary Magdalene and Zacchaeus. (5) As they were changed they could enjoy the Messiah's presence and the blessings of the dawning Messianic Age. But the Holy Spirit still had to come. (6) Those who received this promise (7) from the Father after Jesus was glorified experienced the Holy Spirit living within them, closer even than the physical Jesus had been. Touched by His Power alive in them, the Living Waters of the Spirit bubbled up in them out of the depths of their hearts – from the very depths and mainspring of their beings. And the joy of it all was that, as Peter explained on the Day of Pentecost, the promise was for everyone. (8)

Is anyone thirsty, empty, dissatisfied, or in need of a change of direction? Jesus still speaks to us today, so why not take that leap of faith, whether we are already committed to the Lord or not, and come to Him asking Him to fill us and refill us? We need to be filled daily with His Spirit to keep our relationship with the Lord fresh and alive, just as we have to renew our human relationships from time to time. We can all receive more of the Spirit. Most of us drink too little liquid to keep us healthy. So, too, spiritually. Many of us are satisfied with an occasional nod in the direction of The Almighty! If we want a real encounter, however, our relationship with God cannot be an extra option. It must be an all-absorbing business. If we are truly filled with the Living Water of the Spirit it will bubble up out of the depths of our hearts and shine out of our faces. We will want Him to continue to satisfy us, fill us, carry us along amid the problems of life and affect others. We shall be 'a new creation' ready to attend the Wedding Feast.

See, the streams of living waters,

Springing from eternal love,

Well supply thy sons and daughters,

And all fear of want remove:

Who can faint while such a river

Ever flows their thirst to assuage?

Grace, which like the Lord the Giver,

Never fails from age to age. (9)

To think through:

i.   What do we need if we are spiritually thirsty, empty, dissatisfied with life and in need of a change of direction?

ii.   Why do we need to "be filled daily with His Holy Spirit"?

iii. If anyone has had an experience of being filled with the Spirit, thank God for it and try to share the experience with a group of Christians, but no-one should feel under obligation to do so. This is a liberating experience, not to be seen as creating a "them and us" situation.

(1)   See Ezekiel 47 vv 1 et al, Zechariah 14 vv 8-9.
(2)   See Leviticus 23 vv 33-43.
(3)   Isaiah 55 v 1.
(4)   Isaiah 44 vv 3-4.
(5)   See Luke 5 vv 1-11; Luke 8 v 2; Luke 19 vv 1-10.
(6)   See Acts 1 v 8.
(7)   See Acts 2 onwards.
(8)   See Acts 2 v 21.
(9)   English Hymnal 393 v 2.

III   THE DEMANDS OF THE KINGDOM I

INTRODUCTION

Encounter with the living Christ demands certain changes in our old lifestyle. At whatever stage we are along the Way, there will always be occasions when we can benefit from rethinking our attitudes.

1.   REPENTANCE: THE PRODIGAL SON

(Luke 15 vv 11-32.)

"Father, give me my share of the estate"... "This son of mine was... lost and is found" (verses 12 and 24).

* * * * * * *

Two lads playing around Rouen Cathedral in France decided to make a hoax confession as a practical joke, with all the most preposterous sins they could think up! The priest's advice, to one of the boys anyway, was to go and kneel before the life-size Crucifix in the Cathedral, which he did. There, he was so overwhelmed by the generosity of a God Whose Love for His people allowed His Son to die to save us from evil, that he was truly brought to his senses. He came home to His Father in deep repentance. That boy later became Archbishop of Rouen! (1)...

Everyone knows the story. A wastrel younger son asked for his share of the family fortune and his father, in his wisdom, gave it to him. The young man set off for a country as far away from his home as possible. Having squandered all his money on wine, women and song, this wastrel found himself in that ignominious and disgraceful position, for a Jew, of feeding pigs, which were unclean animals according to them, as a hired servant, without receiving even a morsel of food. In that very moment, as an outcast, he realised the stark contrast of his degraded situation in comparison with the love he had taken for granted in his father's house where even the hired servants fared better. So he came to his senses, like that French Archbishop had done, determined to return home, seeking forgiveness and asking to be counted as one of his father's hired servants!

Here is a parable about the 'world'. God created a world with certain Laws, for our own well-being, yet with freedom of approach to God and freedom of choice. (2) Like the younger son, we have all abused that freedom which our loving Heavenly Father gave us, taking our share and squandering it. Here, in the West, many people have lived a lifestyle far beyond what is a fair share of the 'fortune', as have other affluent societies and rulers in the world. Indeed, from time immemorial there have been extravagant rulers and subjects from a Solomon to a Shah in Persia. Political leaders and their régimes, as well as the Church at times, in many countries today continue the same extravagance whilst their subjects suffer starvation in the most abject of conditions. We continue to live extravagantly today despite the warnings of drought, famine, climate change, and at the expense of our poorer brothers and sisters. When we have used our resources then we shall be like that wastrel younger son. But the rape of Mother Earth cannot go on. Let us come to our senses before it is too late. (3) The Aboriginals in Australia have much to teach us on the sacred nature of the earth both in their respect for the land and in the way they manage the ecology – even if from a different perspective.

Yet, like that earthly father who waited and watched for any signs of his son's return, so, too, God waits and watches for us. That earthly father was generous in the extreme – extravagantly so, just as our Heavenly Father is. God still gives to us abundantly, meeting us, too, while we are still far off, with Love and forgiveness. He longs for us all to have these good things and has already prepared a Wedding Feast for us at the cost of His Son's life. So He asks those of us who have more of the fortune and goodies, like the elder son, to share with those who have so little or none. We have at the same time been both the wastrel younger son and the elder son, jealously guarding everything for ourselves.

Lord, help us to come to our senses as we contemplate Your Love and generosity, both in the abundant resources we have and receive from the Third World. Show us each ways in which we can stop squandering our share and guarding it jealously, and at the same time, ensure a fairer distribution throughout the world.

To think through:

i.   In what ways have we in the West abused the freedom that God has given us? How can our raping of Mother Earth, taking more than our share, squandering it and living a lifestyle far beyond what is our share of the fortune be reconciled by those who call themselves Christians? [A look at a book such as *The Earth From The Air* by Yann Arthus-Bertrand (Thames and Hudson 1992/2002) is extremely helpful and hopefully could be borrowed from a library.]

ii. If we continue to live extravagantly and to despoil our world with carbon emissions, what will the inevitable consequences be (a) for us (b) for our poorer brothers and sisters? We need to look at this in terms of spiritual, mental, emotional and physical as well as social consequences. What would God have us do?

iii. How can we be said to be at the same time both the wastrel younger son and the jealous elder brother? And why is it that God does not give up on us?

52

(1)   Source untraceable.
(2)   See Genesis 2 vv 16 and 17; Ephesians 2 v 18; and Hebrews
        4 v 16.
(3)   See Deuteronomy 30 vv 19 and 20.

2.   HUMILITY: INSTRUCTIONS ON GOING TO AND GIVING

PARTIES

(Luke 14 vv 7-14.)

"Everyone who exalts himself will be humbled, and he who humbles himself will be exalted" (verse 11).

* * * * * * *

As a child I remember him walking along in a pair of old trousers with a lawn-mower slung across his shoulders, on his way to mow the lawn for what in those days was known as the 'Unmarried Mothers' and Babies' Home', which was temporarily without a gardener. Here was a Bishop, yet he was always willing to share the lot of the outcast, to do menial tasks. A man of prayer, whose love and relationship with Christ enabled him to be truly at everyone's disposal, totally unconcerned about himself. You knew you were talking to a humble saint and one's life was the richer for it.

One Sabbath, when dining with an eminent Pharisee and his learned friends, Jesus noticed their lack of humility and compassion as they watched critically to accuse Him if He healed a poor man suffering from dropsy. So, when He did heal him, He reminded them that, although they would rescue humans and animals on the Sabbath, (1) yet they would not allow a man to be healed.

Jesus also noticed their lack of humility as they jockeyed for the places of honour on arrival. Rather, it seemed, than upset His host He illustrated how they should behave by a parable. He chose an occasion they would all attend sometimes – a wedding, where He saw them seeking the places of honour. That a wedding was also a symbol of the Messianic Age was significant! He suggested that on arrival they should not take the best places lest more important people than they came. Then with what shame would they have to move down! Jesus saw the host as recognising the fact that a guest had placed himself in a lowly position by saying "Friend" rather than a peremptory "give place"... They ought to have read Proverbs carefully! (2) And indeed He suggested that hosts should invite the the poor, the crippled, the lonely, the lame and the blind.

Exalting oneself, making much of oneself, is rebellion against God. Judas put himself above Jesus when he thought he knew better than Him in trying to force Him to declare Himself as Messiah. (3) Even James and John vied for position in the Kingdom. (4) Jesus, however, "did not come to be served, but to serve" (5) and set the example by washing the disciples' feet. (6) He came also "to give his life as a ransom for many". (5)

When power corrupts, whole peoples are subdued or obliterated. The ordinary folk could barely exist under Pharisaic domination. The masses starve in countries where rulers want all the power and wealth for themselves. In recent years we have seen Emperors fall, Governments topple and dictators assassinated because of their corruption, with appalling consequences for their people.

In God's Kingdom attitude to position is reversionary – in other words, the world's standards are turned upside down. Amid a greedy and violent world what is it that really impresses people? A little saint on the streets of Calcutta – Mother Teresa – with the poorest of the poor, the unloved, the unlovely and the dying; a nun taking the place of another in the gas chamber...a cross set on a hill. Such an action, where a Man loved enough to die for each one of us, is enough to melt the heart of the most redoubtable sinner.

Self-aggrandisement, putting oneself first, repels. Humility, however, recognises God's Sovereignty and draws people to Him like a magnet. Jesus suggested that our socialising should include inviting the poor, downtrodden and outcasts of our society rather than those whom we like, who are influential or can invite us back. Here is a real service and washing of people's feet rather than offering charity handouts at a distance. Such humility would offer the Kingdom to those who would otherwise have little or no chance to receive it.

Lord, please help me to overcome my pride. I want to surrender my heart to You and place myself at the disposal of those who are the least of Your brethren in the eyes of the world.

To think through:

i.   In this parable Jesus saw the host as recognising the fact that a guest had placed himself in a lowly position by saying "friend" as opposed to the more peremptory "give way". (See Proverbs 25 vv 6-7, which the Pharisees had neglected to take note of!) When could we expect to hear Jesus say "friend" to us? (No quick answer can be sought here.)

ii.   Think of examples in the Bible where people have exalted themselves, tried to vie for position in the Kingdom, been puffed up with pride or sought self-aggrandisement. (See Mark 10 vv 35-45; Acts 5 vv 1-11; Acts 12 vv 21-24; and III John vv 9-10.) What does Jesus or the Church have to say about such situations?

iii. In God's Kingdom attitude to position is reversionary. Amid a greedy and violent world how can a Cross set on a hill still claim to be the epitome of humility? How does each of us see real service and what does such service do for those whose feet we are washing, and for us?

iv.   Who are the outcasts and despised around you?

(1)   See Deuteronomy 22 v 4.
(2)   See Proverbs 25 vv 6 and 7.
(3)   See Matthew 26 vv 14 and 15; Mark 14 vv 10 and 11; Luke 22 vv 3-6.
(4)   See Mark 10 vv 35-45.
(5)   Mark 10 v 45; see also Matthew 20 vv 20-28; compare Luke 22 vv 24-30.
(6)   See John 13 vv 1-17.

3.   PERSISTENCE: THE FRIEND AT MIDNIGHT

(Luke 11 vv 1-10. See also Matthew 7 vv 7-12; Mark 11 v 24; John

15 vv 7 and 16; 16 vv 23 and 24.)

"My friend, lend me three loaves"… "I tell you…persistence will be enough to make him get up and give his friend all he wants" (vv 6a and 8b, Jerusalem Bible).

* * * * * * *

One night I was awakened by my telephone bell ringing. When I eventually answered it there was a friend asking for help. Her persistent and beseeching tone made me repent of my mixed feelings at being aroused so abruptly. I just had to go to her assistance, otherwise I would have had her on my mind and I knew that I would be failing the Lord not to help someone in need. Such a persistent request had set in motion the necessary requisites for prayer to be answered – asking in the belief that I would help.

The disciples had asked Jesus to teach them how to pray, as the Rabbis and John the Baptist had taught their disciples. They were impressed by the spontaneity and freshness of His prayer, like His teaching. (1) The result was that priceless pattern for us, the Lord's Prayer, (2) transcending all Jewish concepts and teaching. Then by means of an amusing parable He taught them how important persistence in praying was for their relationship with God and for making their requests to Him. The man showed that his need for bread was genuine and sincere, inconvenient as it was for his friend, who nonetheless answered his plea for the sake of his sleeping family, tucked in as they would have been by one large blanket.

God longs to give us what we sincerely and genuinely ask for because He loves us and not because He tires of hearing our petitions, or wishes to be shot of us – like the man in bed! No, He already knows them, much as parents do when a child pleads for what he or she wants for a birthday present. Or like the lady in an iron lung who praised God so continuously and earnestly that she was healed. By our persistence we build up a two-way relationship, showing that our desires are indeed genuine and that we are quietly trusting Him to provide the answer, which He always does sooner or later, whether it is yes, no or wait. This is different from badgering God and demanding that He grants us what we ask for ***and*** in the way we want, which ignores His Sovereignty. God's unfailing promise is, "ASK and it will be GIVEN to you; SEEK and you WILL FIND. KNOCK and the door will be OPENED to you…" (3)

We are tired, easily distracted, there's a train to catch, the telephone is ringing, the baby is crying, the children are late for school, there's the shopping. The devil uses these occasions to crowd God out of our lives and all too soon we have given up on our prayer and requests. We become faint-hearted and soon we can no longer easily communicate with God or hear what He is saying. We become divorced from Him Who is the "ground of our being". (4)

The need for persistence in prayer is vital if we wish to maintain our relationship with God, receive what we long for and listen for His Word. Rooted and grounded in Him we can then pray with quiet confidence that He will respond to our prayers, just as the man in the parable was sure that his friend would answer.

58

Father, give us that gift of persistence in our relationship with You and in making our requests so that all men may know Your Salvation and Your Kingdom be enlarged.

<u>*To think through*</u>:

i.   How is persistence different from badgering God? What does such badgering fail to recognise? What do we build up by persistence?

ii.   For what shall we ask and hope to receive; seek and hope to find; knock and hope to find opened? (Hope in the New Testament is almost equivalent to belief.) There may be some heart-searching and surprises here! How can we really ask in faith, seek earnestly and knock until we get what we believe God wants for us? What is God looking for in our persistence?

iii.   What things militate against and prevent us from constancy in prayer? Why are these things useful to the devil?

(1)   See Mark 1 vv 21-28.
(2)   See VI B1.
(3)   Matthew 7 vv 7 and 8.
(4)   St Augustine of Hippo.

4.   GIVING GENEROUSLY: THE MEASURE YOU GIVE WILL
BE THE MEASURE YOU GET

Luke 6 v 38. See also Matthew 7 v 1&2 and Mark 4 v 24

"Give, and it will be given to you. A good measure, pressed down, shaken together and running over, will be poured into your lap" (Luke 6 v 38).

* * * * * * *

Some friends of mine, living a life of faith and trust in God, gave the savings they had, with little hope of return, to someone in need. A few days before their holiday they still had no money but they trusted Jesus and that He would supply their needs. At the eleventh hour a friend, totally unaware of their plight, handed them an envelope saying, "I've been meaning to give you this for some time to help with your bills." It was the exact amount of their holiday – and a little more besides!

Giving and receiving are like the ebb and flow of the tide. Jesus illustrated this principle in the parable of the measure used for weighing corn. You can see the joy of the Kingdom percolating through. The measure you give will be the measure you get back, "good measure, pressed down, shaken together", with more to come, "running over" and "poured into your lap" (the voluminous folds of a Jewish robe where the gleanings were put). An overflowing abundance.

The Kingdom has this principle built into it. Jesus **_gave_** His life for our Salvation and we **_receive_** Eternal life, abundantly. The more we give ourselves to Him, the more we receive of His precious gifts – the gifts of the Spirit like preaching, teaching, leadership, healing and prophecy. (1) All these are for use in His service to gather a great harvest of souls, until we all attain "to the whole measure of the fulness of Christ". (2) We are stewards of all the gifts and talents He gives us,

60

gratefully received. Like a cypress tree which puts forth its branches for shade, so the gifts that come our way we should spread out for others to receive.

Yes, God intends us to share joyfully what we have as Zacchaeus did when he received Salvation. (3) However Jesus warned us that riches could bind and exclude one from the Kingdom, like the Rich Young Ruler, (4) the Rich Fool (5) and the miser in Ben Jonson's *Volpone* who worshipped his gold secretly and gained troubles innumerable! The Good News of the Kingdom can be shocking indeed for the rich and not so rich alike, for it unhinges us from that to which we seek to cling. Our relationship with Jesus should put wealth in its proper perspective, freeing us from bondage to money and possessions and giving us joy when we see others receiving what we already so richly have.

The measure we give is to be the very best we have of our time, energy, talents and abilities, our food, money and resources – our very lives. In this way we honour and thank Jesus for the most costly gift of Salvation and recognise God's Sovereignty over us. Our Heavenly Father wants to give us His Holy Spirit and all good gifts. (6) And He does, but, as in farming, "whoever sows sparingly will also reap sparingly, and whoever sows generously will also reap generously." (7)

Often we find that the poorer the person or country, the more proportionately generous is their giving, which should say something to the less poor among us. (8) Generous giving leaves us open to receive all that the good Lord wants to give us – good measure and running over, the joy of the Kingdom expressed in terms of the joy of a Wedding Feast.

Father, we thank You for all Your gifts, especially the gift of Your Son and His Spirit. We ask You that we may respond to what we have received and allow Your abundance to spill over to others that they may receive the same joy.

**To think through**:

i. As we give more and more of ourselves to God and to others in His service (read Matthew 25 vv 31-46) what gifts do you think we shall receive in return? For what purpose are we given those gifts (read Ephesians 4 vv 7-13) and in what ways can we become blinded by such gifts?

ii. How is it that so often the poorer the person or country, the more generous (proportionately) is their giving?

iii. Generous giving leaves us open to receive all that the Father wants to give us. What would you like to receive from Him?

(1) See Romans 12 vv 6-8; I Corinthians 12 vv 4-11; Ephesians 4 vv 7-13.

(2) Ephesians 4 v 13.

(3) See Luke 19 vv 1-10.

(4) See Luke 18 vv 18-30.

(5) See Luke 12 vv 13-21.

(6) See Luke 11 v 13.

(7) II Corinthians 9 v 6.

(8) See Matthew 10 v 8.

5.   FAITH: THE LILIES OF THE FIELD

(Matthew 6 vv 25-34; Luke 12 vv 22-31.)

"Therefore, I tell you, do not worry about your life, what you will eat or drink... But seek first his kingdom and his righteousness, and all these things will be given to you as well" (Matthew 6 vv 25 and 33).

* * * * * * *

Two contrasting scenes. First, a lovely summer's day and we are enraptured by a beautiful vista. Suddenly we feel in harmony with God and the universe. Not a care in the world! By contrast a snowbound area in winter can lead to anxiety and worry over food and drink, clothing and heating...

Jesus here gives us a picture of the calm orderliness of Creation as Genesis states existed in Eden, with mutual trust between God and man before Adam and Eve sinned. (1) Then fear and insecurity crept in and a painful separation from God. (2) It is humbling for us to know that Nature quietly gets on with life and is fed and nurtured by God Who cares for the whole of His Creation, which is more resplendent by far than ever wealthy Solomon was!

Sin, greed and a grasping attitude to wealth, all bring anxiety and worry in their wake and are self-destructive. They cannot contribute to our growth but they can bring about neurosis and physical illness, thus hastening our end. They are sins against God's Sovereignty, showing a lack of trust in His loving care and are useless. Of themselves they cannot alter the past, present or future. They cripple us and prevent us from getting on with life. Sometimes people find themselves anxious for no obvious reason, yet this must stem from a fallen world in and around us... How often Jesus greeted His disciples with words like "Why are you so afraid? Do you still have no faith?" (3)

Faith, the antidote to worry, acknowledges God's Sovereignty over the universe and seeks "first his kingdom and his righteousness", knowing that "all these things will be added" for a worry-free life in spirit, mind and body.

Sadly, however, God is all too often impeded from fulfilling our needs. This is because firstly we do not always appropriate our Salvation and our Kingdom-status – hence many remain in bondage. Furthermore cosmic sin, rebellion and ignorance affect Christian and non-Christian, sinner and sinned against alike. So one finds _**spiritual**_ anguish, hunger and restlessness; _**mental**_ distress and minds polluted by evil, crime and violence; and _**bodies**_ either over-indulged or under-fed through ignorance, greed and vested interests. Yet there are Spiritual and earthly resources enough for all the world's needs if only we would put into practice the ethics of the Kingdom and bring pressure to bear on world Governments to pay attention to all three aspects of human life – to body, mind and spirit, to provide for healthy, whole people – their basic human right.

Ours is the responsibility as Christians of seeking God's Kingdom and His Righteousness afresh for ourselves and for the whole world for "No man is an island...each is part of the whole." (4) By proclaiming the Gospel we can help to bring Salvation and freedom to millions enslaved by worry and anxiety, and unable to help themselves without Christ. We can also pray that God's Holy Spirit will shower gifts and blessings on us and them, setting _**spirits**_ free to approach God, (5) asking whatsoever things are needful in Jesus' Name; (6) renewing and freeing _**minds**_ from slavery to past, present and future; meeting _**bodily**_ needs everywhere PROVIDED that we are prepared to share earth's resources and riches.

Then we, with our brothers and sisters throughout the world, may indeed inherit the abundant blessings of the Kingdom, and the morrow will take care of itself.

Lord, in Your mercy, help us this day to seek afresh Your Kingdom and its Laws for ourselves and the world. Amen.

Said the robin to the sparrow, "I would really like to know,

Why these restless human beings rush about and worry so."

Said the sparrow to the robin, "Friend, I think that it must be

That they have no Heavenly Father such as cares for you and me." (7)

To think through:

i.   What are the consequences of cosmic sin? Does this account for the fact that sometimes people find themselves anxious for no obvious reason? If so, where does this stem from?

ii.   In what ways do sin, greed and wealth bring anxiety, worry and self-destruction in their wake? How are they sins against God's Sovereignty and how do they militate for evil against us and prevent God from fulfilling our needs?

iii. What are "all these things" that will be added to those who "seek first "God's" kingdom and His righteousness"? How shall we seek His Kingdom and His righteousness and what does it involve for us?

(1)   See Genesis 3 vv 1-7.
(2)   See Genesis 3 vv 8-25.
(3)   See Mark 4 v 40.
(4)   John Donne *Devotions* XVII.
(5)   See Hebrews 4 v 16.
(6)   See John 15 vv 7-16; 16 vv 23 and 24.
(7)   *Overheard in an Orchard*, from "Can she see?" by E. Cheney (Mowbrays 1996 / Continuum).

6. TWO KINDS OF LOVE: MARTHA AND MARY

(Luke 10 vv 38-42.)

"Martha, Martha, you are anxious and troubled about many things; one thing is needful. Mary has chosen the good portion, which shall not be taken away from her" (verse 42) (Revised Standard Version).

* * * * * * *

The two sisters, Martha and Mary, lived together with their brother Lazarus. Evidently Martha and Mary were much involved in their own housework, whether they had servants or not. On this occasion Mary seems to have neglected her share of the work and left Martha to carry on alone! This quite naturally upset Martha, but Jesus seems to have sensed something else. "Martha, Martha, you are anxious and troubled about many things." Mary has chosen the good part: Martha was doing a good job, but she was worrying and fussing, getting flustered. He may have noticed a tinge of jealousy and anger that Mary was where she would like to have been, but felt the meal was more important then. Or He may have felt that Martha liked the fuss and worry because it fulfilled a need in her. Yet she was so busy that she really hadn't taken time to be with Jesus, and soon He would be gone. She needed to get her priorities right.

Mary, however, like the disciples of a Rabbi, realised that she needed to spend time with Jesus, getting to know His thoughts and teachings, and offering her costliest love. (1) Jesus commended her for this, for she was drinking deeply of the cup of Love and being filled.

In India it is quite common for people to watch holy men meditating and just being with them. What are they learning? Not just to see how he combs his hair but to discover how he came to be filled with peace. In the 1960s and 1970s it became fashionable for people like the Beatles to race off to India to find a guru and to try to find themselves and gain an inner strength.

Jesus makes it clear that we do not need to leave our jobs or even to rush off to the furthermost parts of the earth to learn secret mantras and meditations to find peace. We can find it here, in our midst. If we care to spend even a few minutes each day just sitting in His presence, reflecting on His life and teaching, we shall keep in touch and harmony with Him and fill ourselves with the cleansing power of His forgiveness. Then His Love, peace and grace can percolate our lives and fulfil every need, sufficient for the tasks of the day without our getting flustered. Maybe sometimes we can go on a retreat to recharge our batteries more completely. If Jesus needed to pray constantly and withdraw at times, how much more do we need to do so? Others will then notice the difference such contact with Him makes to us (like seeing Moses' face shine after being on the mountain with God). (2) They will be drawn to Jesus to find the same calm pools of peace for their souls and we shall indeed be of service to God in the advancement of His Kingdom towards that Eternal Wedding Feast.

Lord, help us to realise that it is only by looking at You that we shall truly be able to reflect Your Glory and so draw others to You as they realise the source of our power.

To think through:

i.   Even amid a busy life what is the most important thing for a Christian and how can this be achieved?

ii.   What do you think would be the benefits of going on a retreat and spending time alone with the Lord (either in silence, semi-silence or a time of shared reflection with other Christians)?

iii.   Would you find such an experiment repressive? If so, why? What might happen in the silence?

(1)   See John 12 v 3.
(2)   See Exodus 34 vv 29-35.

7.   SPIRITUAL HUNGER: "BLESSED ARE THOSE WHO

HUNGER AND THIRST FOR RIGHTEOUSNESS"

(Matthew 5 v 6. See also Luke 6 vv 21 and 24-25.)

"Blessed are those who hunger and thirst for righteousness, for they will be filled" (Matthew 5 verse 6).

* * * * * * *

At the heart of the Beatitudes stands the necessity of hungering and thirsting, not like the physical hunger and thirst that we may experience but an intense longing with all of one's heart, mind and soul. It is a yearning for God's Righteousness, for His Salvation and wholeness and for the establishment of His Kingdom in ourselves and others. God's call to the Israelites who hungered and thirsted for Him (1) was taken further by Jesus. He alone can appease our hunger, for He is the Bread of Life. (2) He alone can quench our thirst, for He is "a spring of water welling up to eternal life". (3)

There are many sects today within Christianity. Some are Pharisaic and exclusive in their approach to membership of the Kingdom. As throughout history, the last two centuries have also seen systems opposed to Christianity, like Marxism which seeks to bring about a peaceful and just society by whatever means. But these are not the Kingdom. The criterion for those who follow Christ, however, is to discover (a) what the Kingdom means and (b) what Laws there are.

(a)   Jesus came to earth to establish God's Kingdom and Reign wherein Righteousness and Truth can flourish (4) "not by might, nor by power, but by my Spirit". (5) Only God is wholly Righteous but this is more than moral perfection. It is Holiness or Wholeness, perfect Harmony and Love. Jesus fulfilled these attributes of God, revealed first by the Prophets, in His Life and Death. And we, if we are governed by His Love, will be seeking to bring in His Reign, yearning for His

Righteousness and Holiness to be established in our hearts. We shall need to long for the Holy Spirit to fill us and replenish us daily. The more we long for Him to possess us and fill us with the fruit of the Spirit, the more He will change us.

(b)   The Pharisees believed that if they kept the letter of the Law even for a day, or fulfilled all Righteousness perfectly, then the Kingdom would come. But Jesus said "Unless your righteousness surpasses that of the Pharisees…you will certainly not enter the kingdom…"(6) What does Jesus mean and require? A totally different form of Righteousness – keeping God's Holy Law of Love. And for this we need to be changed and born again, as He told Nicodemus. (7)

When we have found the Pearl of Great Price, (8) Who alone can satisfy and bless us, then we shall want with all our hearts and minds and souls to see that His Kingdom is announced to everyone. Never may we be satisfied with allowing the state of things as they are in the world but rather strive whole-heartedly to share the Good News that Jesus has triumphed over evil which need have no more hold over anyone. "Utopia" you say? No, but rather the Golden Age, prophesied by Isaiah, (9) established in everyone's heart and fulfilled for us in the Wedding Feast of the Lamb Who has redeemed the world.

> *"Now the dwelling of God is with men, and he will live with them. They will be his people, and God himself will be with them and be their God." (10)*

To think through:

i.   How can we "hunger and thirst for righteousness"?

ii.   How can God's Righteousness be established in our hearts?

iii.   Why are there still so many men and women of violence? How can we help to reduce the number?

(1)   See Isaiah 55 v 1.
(2)   See John 6 vv 32-51.
(3)   John 4 v 14.
(4)   See Psalms 85 vv 10-13; 86 v 11 et al.
(5)   Zechariah 4 v 6.
(6)   Matthew 5 v 20.
(7)   See John 3 vv 1-15.
(8)   See Matthew 13 vv 45-6.
(9)   See Isaiah 11 vv 1-10.
(10)   Revelation 21 v 3.

IV   THE SECRET GROWTH OF THE KINGDOM

INTRODUCTION – TRANSFIGURATION

(See Mark 9 vv 2-9; Matthew 17 vv 1-13 and Luke 9 vv 28-36.)

Encounter with Jesus brings great joy and encouragement. We feel different and know His presence in our lives in a wonderful way. Yet the greatest changes often occur only with faithful perseverance and endurance, quietly and secretly, almost unnoticed, like seeds growing. Within God's Kingdom there is a secret, hidden development towards a climax in God's own time. Just as Jesus was transfigured so, too, the heart of the Gospel for a disciple is a transfiguring experience of being changed from glory to glory.

To think through:

i.   How was the Transfiguration important a) for Jesus and b) for His disciples?

ii.   What does it mean to be transfigured?

iii. Why do you think that some people believe Jesus' Transfiguration might have happened after His Resurrection?

1.   THE SOWER

(Mark 4 vv 1-20; Matthew 13 vv 1-9 and 18-23; Luke 8 vv 4-15.)

"The sower sows the word" (Mark 4 v 14) (Revised Standard Version).
"The seed is the word of God" (Luke 8 v 11).

* * * * * * *

Anyone who is interested in finance knows precisely how precarious investment in the Stock Market is! Some funds are more stable than others, so I'm told that people place a certain amount of money there and speculate for a high yield with the rest if the Market is viable!.

Farming in Jesus' day in Palestine was rather like this. The sower would scatter seeds from his bag as he walked up and down the strips of land. They would fall randomly along the pathways, rocks and among the thorns as well as the good soil. An element of risk was involved.

Jesus is saying that God is like the sower. There is that same element of risk, even waste, when He sows the Word in people's hearts, according to the response of the receiver. He knows that His Word, Jesus, will be received in different ways:-

Take the pathway, for instance, with no depth of soil. How typical of many people who hear the Word, yet there is no depth to their conversion. They do not allow the Word to penetrate the recesses of their spirits and evil still has a stronghold. They never really make up their minds either, about God and Jesus, or any other subject. Any form of religion, or none, will do. Yes, they hear, but are deaf to the call.

Or there's the rocky soil where the Word is received joyously and active growth takes place, yet God's Word cannot mature because there's no root. In times of trouble such people have no anchor to keep themselves rooted and grounded in Christ. There may be some who find an echoing note here. We have all known such times and perhaps found it difficult to hold on in faith. We wonder what God is up to and whether He has deserted us. Like Job we wish to hold on, protesting our innocence, yet we vent our anger and frustration on God and other people. God can take it, but instead of leaving it with Him some of us become bitter and resentful, rejecting Him.

What of the thorny ground? Yes, the Word is quickly and joyfully received, too but soon overgrown. It is all too easy to get caught up in the swing of life, of materialism and wealth. A two income family, an upmarket house, with extensions. One has to keep up with the Jones', the go-getters and yuppies, or trendsetters. Fine, but all too often one becomes ruled by "the more I have, the more I want" principle. People in this type of soil can be too absorbed in the cares and worries of this life to notice God and His Kingdom.

We may recognise, or partially recognise ourselves somewhere along the line. But there is Good News. Inasmuch as we allow the Holy Spirit free play in our lives we can make that response to God's Word which will ensure our growth in the good soil. We must allow Him to dig deep so that, like the man who built his house on the rock, we will be able to lay our foundations (1) and stand firm on that Rock which will endure through crises, and enable us to resist all that is not of the

Gospel. The more deeply rooted our lives are in the Word, the higher
our spiritual yield, thirty-, sixty-, even a hundred-fold.

Lord, alas that much of our soul's soil is poor,

Through ignorance, carelessness and sin.

Yet You give us the remedy -

To dig deep into Your Word to lay our foundations aright.

To think through:

i.   What sort of people are represented by the four soils? Do any of
      the soils speak to the situation in our lives?

ii.   How can we be sure that we receive the Good News and ensure
      growth in the good soil?

iii. What does "He who has ears to hear" mean? What prevents our
      hearing God's Word?

(1)   See Matthew 7 vv 24-27.

2.   THE SEED GROWING SECRETLY

(Mark 4 vv 26-29.)

"This is what the kingdom of God is like. A man scatters seed on the ground. Night and day, whether he sleeps or gets up, the seed sprouts and grows, though he does not know how" (verses 26 and 27).

* * * * * * *

Possibly many of us have planted beans in a jar and watched with growing excitement first the beans dying off, then the slow but sure and steady growth of new shoots, not knowing how that growth is achieved.

Yet the Kingdom of God's growth is more exhilarating by far than this. The whole dramatic act of Creation pulsated with Divine Love and energy, shot through with moments of delight. (1) God's Spirit moved, or hovered, through space, laying the foundations of His Universe (2) until at length He created man in His own image, (3) and endowed him with spirit, or the potential to be eternal, like God, and with the ability to propagate or reproduce, like the seeds that the farmer sowed. The fruit of His labour is reflected in the reciprocal relationship He appeared to have with Adam and Eve. Such joy is normal in the life of the Kingdom. (4)

The secret growth of His Kingdom is God's own Divine Sovereign mystery. In the first place He put His natural Law within each person's heart, (5) but in His Wisdom He also gave man freedom to choose to delight in Him and His Love, which is Heaven (Kingdom living) or to be alienated from Him, which is hell. (6) Yet inbuilt into the very plan of Creation God has provided a way back, which brings one into an even closer and more mature relationship than our primal Paradisiacal status could. Freewill, which God knew was potentially dangerous, is also the means by which mankind is saved. God sent Jesus to show us the nature of true love and to bring free will to its crowning glory, in His freely laying down His Life for us and instead of us. In doing so He brought forth many fruits and blessings. God's Reign is restored in our lives in a new and dynamic way, the old yielding to the new in mystical death. Our old sinful lives are buried by Baptism into His Death and raised to new life through His Resurrection. (7)

God has always been watching over His Creation, but with the coming of Jesus there was a new sense of urgency. When Jesus, the Seed or Word of God, died there was an almighty explosion, like dynamite, when the gates of hell were burst asunder and God's forces of life and light reclaimed control, with all those who had died before Jesus' Death having the Gospel preached to them. (8) Like the farmer, God had done His work of sowing. Then the seed had to take root and germinate, and indeed the spiritual power at work in the Resurrection and coming of the Holy Spirit produced a mighty harvest of souls. (9)

Over the centuries this work of planting and germinating has been going on quietly through those first disciples, whose witness reached countless numbers of people and, who in turn began to spread the Word to the uttermost part of the earth, to take root there, even to our own day.

Mercifully God still waits and watches over the Word He has sown in each of us today, through our Conversion, Dedication, Baptism or through whatever way He chooses to come to us. Even if little or nothing appears to be happening, God is still on His throne, active in Creation, His Spirit hovering over it, and at the Divinely appointed time, perhaps after years of patient waiting, that seed will have died sufficiently for it to burst forth, exploding with vibrant new spiritual life.

The growth of the Kingdom in individuals and in the world at large is often quiet and unspectacular and sometimes more obvious through the Holy Spirit's activity and through intercessory prayer. The fruits of Jesus' Death and Resurrection are with us today, burgeoning even in seemingly unlikely corners. May we be among those first fruits at His Wedding Feast.

76

Lord, we thank You that Your plan for us in Creation is an unlimited one in which we are called to share in the fruits of Redemption, to bring about a mighty harvest for Your Kingdom.

To think through:

i. Why is it that growth in the Kingdom, in individuals and in the Christian Church is often quiet and unspectacular (though given that there are also outward signs of the Spirit at work)?

ii. Where can we see signs of growth in the Christian Church today? Who is responsible? Does this conflict with the idea of secret growth? If so, what is the difference?

iii. What does the time of secret growth refer to?

(1) See Genesis 1 vv 10, 12, 18, 21a, 22, 25, 31.`
(2) See Genesis 1 v 2.
(3) See Genesis 1 vv 26-30.
(4) See *The New Man*, page 37. Thomas Merton (Burns, Oates 1962).
(5) See Romans 1 vv 18-32.
(6) See Genesis 2 v 16, Deuteronomy 30 v 15-20
(7) See Romans 5 v 6 – 6 v 11; Colossians 3 vv 1-4; et al.
(8) See I Peter 3 vv 18-19; 4 v 6.
(9) See Acts 2 vv 22-41; 3 vv 1-16; et al.

3.   THE MUSTARD SEED

(Mark 4 vv 30-32; Matthew 13 vv 31 and 32; Luke 13 vv 18 and 19.)

"The kingdom of God ... is like a grain of mustard seed, which, when sown upon the ground, is the smallest of all the seeds on earth; yet when it is sown it grows up and becomes the greatest of all shrubs, and puts forth large branches, so that the birds of the air can make nests in its shade" (Mark 4 vv 31-32) (Revised Standard Version).

* * * * * * *

One winter's day a friend of mine planted an orange pip indoors and although England is not the best of climates for growing oranges, we enjoyed watching this seedling grow. An unlikely beginning, yet already within a year or so it became a mighty plant, maturing and shooting out ever more leaves, soon to turn into branches. The Creator Himself must have much the same delight as He watches the slow, often uneven, but steady growth of His Kingdom, despite all the odds of evil forces at work in the world... To the Jew the mustard seed was a source of amusement almost. So small, yet growing to a large bush in which birds could nest. An unlikely beginning, it would seem.

Nothing could have seemed smaller, more insignificant, less promising than the beginnings of Christianity. A small group of faithful followers amongst whom were His twelve Apostles was all Jesus could boast, one of whom betrayed Him, another denied Him, few understood Him, and most of them ran away when He was arrested in the Garden of Gethsemane and before He was crucified. Yet after the Holy Spirit came in power to them on the day of Pentecost (1) these men were changed beyond recognition with boldness and joy. Three thousand people were converted that very day, soon to be followed by a daily increase. The power of the Apostles through the Holy Spirit was enormous. (2)

Gradually it became clear that Salvation was for Gentiles as well. Gentile Godfearers had been present at the feast of Pentecost, (3) and Peter, (4) Stephen, (5) Philip (6) and Barnabas (7) all learned through the Holy Spirit that Gentiles, too, could become Christians. Then, thanks to Paul's vision, (8) Christianity broke free from the burden of Judaism and soon spread throughout the Roman Empire. Later, such was the influence of Christians witnessing under persecution that in 313 A.D. the Emperor Constantine made it the official Imperial religion. He may have had mixed motives and there were obviously dangers inherent in such speedy proselytisation amongst so many different nationals who were ordered to become Christians, rich and poor alike. Yet it ensured the growth and permanence of Christianity. From that time on, through the Dark and Middle Ages, God continued watching over His Kingdom and Christians kept the flame of Light flickering with worship, monasticism, schools, hospitals and evangelisation. Missionaries, like a Columba, a Patrick or a Boniface, spread the Good News far and wide till it reached to the "uttermost part of the earth", (9) often following in the tracks of the explorers as they enlarged the boundaries of the world.

God's Kingdom continues to grow even unto and in our own century. Many people in Africa, South America, Papua New Guinea, China and elsewhere are only now hearing the Good News for the first time. Africa and South America have fast-growing joyful Christians Churches, and those just emerging from cannibalism and head-hunting are accepting Christ with joy. Many miracles and healings are the signs of the workings of the Holy Spirit as He moves over the face of the whole earth. People are no longer becoming Christians because an Emperor decrees it but because the Spirit is breathing into the souls of those who are spiritually hungry in a materialistic age. Evil and intolerance there still is in plenty, yet because of Christ's victory over evil God's Kingdom today is like a rainbow stretching across the world with many different colours of people, shades of belief, and ways of worship – an infinite variety blending into one another, all taking shelter in the branches of the Church, which is the Kingdom of God.

Lord, grant us tolerance to accept the wide variety of peoples who make up Your Church, their different understanding of belief and ways of worship.

To think through:

i. This parable and other stories in the Bible suggest that God likes to work with small numbers and beginnings. Why would this be so? (See for example Judges 6 and 7)

ii. How can God's Kingdom be likened to a rainbow and why?

iii. It is not easy for any family to live together if there are great differences of belief, age and so on. How can the Christian family achieve harmony with so many different races, beliefs, colours and ways of worship?

(1) See Acts 2.
(2) See Acts 2 vv 37-47; 4 vv 4 and 21; 5 vv 12-16.
(3) See Acts 2 v 5.
(4) See Acts 10 and 11.
(5) See Acts 6 v 8 – 7 v 60.
(6) See Acts 8.
(7) See Acts 11 vv 19-26; 13; 14.
(8) See Acts 9 vv 1-31, 13 – 15.
(9) Acts 1 v 8 (Authorised Version).

4.   THE LUMP OF LEAVEN

(Matthew 13 v 33; Luke 13 vv 20-21.)

"The kingdom of heaven is like unto leaven, which a woman took, and hid in three measures of meal, till the whole was leavened" (Matthew 13 verse 33) (Authorised Version).

* * * * * * *

Every cook knows that dough, or yeast, is an important ingredient in baking bread, and that time is needed for it to be proved – to rise. And if the yeast is forgotten – flat, thin bread! Jesus obviously watched Mary cooking very carefully, and He frequently referred to leaven – yeast – so important was it. Leaven is a small piece of dough left over from the previous baking, salted and soured to ferment it. Jewish women knew that if they hid this in their flour when it was fermenting it would 'infect' the flour, acting as a raising agent. This story is the more remarkable since it would have been only a very small lump in this large quantity of flour – three measures as stated in some versions being enough for well over a hundred people! Jesus wanted to show how God prefers to work with small numbers and puny faith. (1) From such small beginnings and little faith God gave the blessings of the Resurrection and the Holy Spirit in superabundance; and from such small beginnings and little faith His Kingdom has exploded into cosmic proportions.

In Jewish society leaven could denote a bad influence. Anything fermenting is really going mouldy. So Jesus warned His disciples about the 'leaven' or influence of the narrow-minded, legalistic Pharisees. (2) And Paul, too, suggested that at Easter, the time of the Jewish Passover, when the old leaven was thrown away, Christians should cast aside "the leaven of malice and wickedness"…for "sincerity and truth". (3)

Leaven, however, also has a cleansing, transforming power as in cooking. "A little leaven leaveneth the whole lump." (4) With a little leaven, just His few intimate disciples, Jesus blazed the trail that transformed individuals, society, the world. And, as we have seen in the parable of the Mustard Seed, that influence has continued throughout the ages…

Today Christianity has suffered in many countries, not least in England, having an Established Church. Though many of our laws were originally based on Christian ethics, alas that today we have almost a sub-culture with Christian laws conforming more and more to what society wants, especially in such matters as divorce, abortion and Sunday trading. Yet even so, with the accent still on the 'little' leaven, the Lord is using that little to fan out to the rest of society and the Holy Spirit is changing lives all over the world. What has remained hidden is even now bearing fruit.

Yes, the fields are ripe unto harvest, and the labourers few. Christians, as the little leaven, have the great privilege and responsibility of acting as raising agents in society, yet we can do so only if our lives are "hidden with Christ in God". (5) Our relationship with Jesus lies in the secret chambers of our hearts, (6) in prayer and in meditating on His Word. What goes on in those secret chambers will shine out in our lives and this is very necessary in an age when people are asking what difference it makes to be a Christian in an ever increasingly multi-faith and secular society. The answer, said Jesus, is "Let your light shine before men, that they may see your good deeds and praise your Father in Heaven." (7)

Lord, may we be like that little lump of leaven, hidden in the midst of society, to spread Your influence in the world and to bring a great harvest of souls into Your Kingdom, so that when You appear in Glory we may be in Glory with You.

To think through:

i.   In what ways was leaven or yeast seen as (a) a good influence and

(b) a bad influence? (Read I Corinthians 5 vv 6-8.)

ii. In what ways should Christians be different from the world?

iii. In what ways has Christianity compromised with the world?

(1)   See, for example, Judges 7.
(2)   See Mark 8 v 15; Matthew 16 v 6; Luke 12 v 1.
(3)   I Corinthians 5 v 8. Authorised Version.
(4)   Ibid.
(5)   Colossians 3 v 3.
(6)   See Matthew 6 v 6.
(7)   Matthew 5 v 16.

5.   THE WHEAT AND THE WEEDS

(Matthew 13 vv 24-30 and 36-43.)

"The kingdom of heaven is like a man who sowed good seed in his field. But while everyone was sleeping his enemy came and sowed weeds among the wheat, and went away. When the wheat sprouted and formed ears, then the weeds also appeared" (verses 24-26).

* * * * * * *

A cornfield of young wheat, looking as if there's not a weed in it, but then, when the ears begin to sprout and ripen, there it is, greyish in colour, spoiling that golden brown look of the wheat... Farmers knew that this insidious darnel weed (the Biblical tare) had to stay there until harvest-time. The roots of both become so intertwined that in pulling up the weeds they might well pull up some precious wheat. However, they were separated at harvest, the darnel being burned and the wheat stored in barns.

Two poles are seen to exist side by side – good and evil. The field represents an innately good world, created by God, but invaded by an evil enemy. God gave man free-will, without which we should be merely puppets, but it led to rebellion. (1) Jesus, however, reclaimed the world for the Father by His healing acts, (2) victorious Death and triumph over evil, (3) thus each one of us is able to overcome evil, too, through Jesus. Yet evil, alas, can look so like good, making it difficult to choose sometimes. So Jesus prayed that His disciples should not be taken out of the world, but kept from the evil one...(4) Why then did Jesus want them in the world?

The answer is that there is still time for change, even for Christians, who as we have already seen, can also act as a raising agent, causing people to change. God alone knows how men will react to influences in their lives. If we accept His Saving Grace, then there is no condemnation, (5) and we pass out of death into life. (6) Yet this transformation is never a blessing for ourselves only but also for sharing the Good News with others, sensitively, lest we make it a stumbling-block. Many will find the Gospel a threat to their old, often more comfortable way of life but we should not be afraid to break down barriers between man and his Creator.

The leavening influence of Christians in society, to which reference was made in the parable of the Lump of Leaven, should be felt and seen in what they believe and in how they behave, especially in situations in which the world would differ from them, like church-going, morals, honesty, social justice and gambling. People should see that Christians are different, not because they are necessarily better, but because they know Christ as their Saviour, and are filled with the Holy Spirit. This 'gentle dew' of the Holy Spirit, seen in Christians, is badly needed in an age where evil stalks through the world and innocent people are at the mercy of satanists, spiritualists, fortune-tellers, men of violence and evil intent; where hijackers and Governments can keep people at bay, even starving, for their own ends ; where life is seen to be cheap and people 'disappear' simply because they are in the way.

Yet evil cannot be plucked away, for change comes secretly, from within, not by a violent, coercing reformation, but through the Holy Spirit gently pervading the world, changing the hearts of rich and poor, young and old, criminal, Communist and Christian alike.

We do not know when the close of the Age will be (7) but Jesus warns us categorically that there will be a Day of Judgment (8) which we have tended to water down, because we believe that God is a loving and merciful God wanting to save everyone. Yet this restricts our free-will and negates the reason for the Incarnation. *__Of course__* He wants everyone to be saved but He cannot compel and those who have never heard the Gospel message will be dealt with mercifully. But for those of us who have heard, we are even now judging ourselves by the measuring line of Jesus. Separation from God is fixed by our own choice but spending Eternity with Him is ours for the asking. (9)

*Thank You Lord that through Your costly Love we may choose
LIFE. "Amen. Come, Lord Jesus." (10)*

To think through:

"The Son of Man will send out His angels, and they will weed out
of His Kingdom everything that causes sin and all who do evil. They
will throw them into the fiery furnace, where there will be weeping
and gnashing of teeth. Then the righteous will shine like the sun in the
Kingdom of their Father." (11)

i.   For what reasons does Jesus want His disciples to live "in the
      world" and yet not be "of the world"?

ii.   What differences can Christians make in the world?

iii. What belief does the Christian Church hold today of a Day of
      Judgment? Has the Gospel teaching been watered down? If
      so, should there be a clearer teaching about it? Does judgment
      conflict with a loving God?

(1)   See Genesis 3 vv 1-7.
(2)   See Luke 4 vv 18-21; 7 vv 18-23; 11 vv 14-23.
(3)   See Colossians 2 vv 14 and 15.
(4)   See John 17 v 15.
(5)   See Romans 8 v 1.
(6)   See John 5 v 24.
(7)   See Mark 13 v 32-37.
(8)   See Matthew 25 vv 31-46; John 5 vv 19-24.
(9)   See John 5 vv 21-29; 10 v 9; 11 v 26.
(10)   Revelation 22 v 20.
(11)   Matthew 13 v 41-43.

6.   THE NET OF FISH

(Matthew 13 vv 47-50.)

"Once again, the kingdom of heaven is like a net that was let down into the lake and caught all kinds of fish. When it was full, the fishermen pulled it up on the shore. Then they sat down and collected the good fish in baskets, but threw the bad away" (verses 47 and 48).

* * * * * * *

Obviously, for Jesus to have told so many parables about the secret and hidden growth of the Kingdom, and two similar parables about two kinds of harvest, suggests the importance of His teaching on it. The double Word from God – like Pharaoh's dreams (1) – means that God will bring it to pass. So, the message concerning the secret mingling of all types of people in the Kingdom and the final separation of good and bad being doubled shows all the urgency of an impending crisis for each individual both now and at the end of time.

The sea with the fish in it represents the world in which there is a great variety of people. The net represents the Kingdom which attracts all sorts and conditions of people, like the dense shoals of fish in the Sea of Galilee, each person having a variety of needs, including Salvation. People, like fish, have to be "caught" – attracted into the Kingdom by the "fishers of men" or disciples. The catch is indiscriminate, like the catch of fish in the net which was dragged along the bottom of the sea; and then the fish were sorted, the good or ceremonially clean from the bad, or ceremonially unclean. (2)

During His Ministry Jesus mingled with every sort of person from Pharisees and Rabbis – the traditionally accepted ceremonially clean – to prostitutes, tax-collectors and sinners – the ceremonially unclean (3) – or those regarded by the Pharisees as beyond hope of Salvation. He came to declare that God loved them as they were and if they accepted His call, then "TODAY, Salvation has come to this house, " (4) bringing about change in their lives.

Like Jesus, Christians are to mingle with all sorts of people, praying that they may influence them by their witness. It is Jesus' task to sort people out finally but it is the task of Christian witnesses, evangelists and preachers to try to bring people into the Kingdom in the power of the Holy Spirit, declaring God's Love for them in that "While we were still sinners", the Father allowed Christ to die for us. (5) And who wouldn't share the knowledge and experience of such a Love that brings blessings to everyone who calls on His Name but in a sensitive way? (6)

The message is urgent because no-one knows when the end of the Age will be. Many, alas, will be totally unprepared, being as afraid of commitment as the fish are of being caught. The net is not yet full despite the Kingdom's growth in some parts of the world. The Good News has not yet reached every heart. So those of us who are His disciples need to be zealous witnesses (but not pushing), lest we fail in our task and we ourselves are excluded from the Wedding Feast.

Yet we shall need to look again at ourselves before being effective witnesses lest we, too, have come to see ourselves as 'ceremonially clean' over against those whom society regards as 'ceremonially unclean' – the drop-outs of our society like the prostitute, the alcoholic, drug-addict, tramp and traveller, the cheat, swindler and crook; yes, even the murderer. These all have the same right of entry as we do. Indeed Kingdom News is reversionary. You can only enter the Kingdom when you know you are on the receiving end of mercy and that you are a spiritual beggar. Such people are only too happy to receive Salvation as a free gift.

*Lord, help us to realise that we are indeed spiritual beggars
when we see what You have done for us who do not deserve it.
And grant that we may return Your Love for us.*

To think through:

i.   Who were the ceremonially unclean in Jesus' day and why? Who might they be today and why?

88

ii.   What is the job of an evangelist, a pastor, a preacher, a missionary?

iii.   Where does their task end and the Lord's begin? (Beware, this is not a trick question but intended to make us think of our different roles)

(1)   See Genesis 41 especially v 32; and IV5.
(2)   See Deuteronomy 14 vv 9 and 10; Leviticus 11 vv 9-12.
(3)   See Mark 2 vv 13-17; 7 vv 1-23; et al.
(4)   Luke 19 v 9.
(5)   Romans 5 v 8.
(6)   See Acts 4 v 12.

7. OF FIG TREES – FRUITFUL AND UNFRUITFUL!

Read:

> (a) Mark 11 vv 12-14 and 20-25; Matthew 21 vv 18-22.
> (b) Luke 13 vv 6-9.
> (c) Mark 13 vv 28-31; Luke 21 vv 29-33.

"Now learn this lesson from the fig tree!" (Mark 13 v 28).

* * * * * * *

In these stories about fig trees we find a common theme – that of Nature's secret growth as winter changes first to spring then to summer, and for which we must watch. If at fruit bearing time a fig tree does not produce figs then it is considered useless and will be cast out… Jesus spoke these parables with the Jewish Nation and Religious leaders in mind, but the meaning is equally applicable to Christians today.

Fig trees in Palestine have always been popular for their shade and succulent fruit and bear two crops yearly in June and September. The first starts in April from the old bark – an indication of something better to come. They are small, hard and inedible then, only ripening in June when the leaves come out fully.

(a)   Whatever the origin of this seemingly enacted parable, here was a fig tree which, despite its leaves shooting forth, was not even bearing those early inedible figs. Although signs of life were apparently there, yet the time of secret growth had borne no fruit. So it did not deserve its glory but rather to be cut down and cast into the fire. (1)

The Pharisees would clearly recognise that Jesus was yet again telling them that they were like whited sepulchres, (2) outwardly looking clean and righteous, yet inwardly dead, bearing no fruit of good works, love and mercy to those who were beyond the pale. The fig tree being **_outside_** Jerusalem was the symbol of a Pharisaic religion that was moribund and must now give way to the New Era. Their slavish obedience to observance made them proud hypocrites, full of deception. What had been going on was more like the growth of a cancer in the nation.

How do Christians stand the same test? Yes, we indulge in good works, church attendance, sick visiting, committees – all the signs of religious life are there. But what of our bickering over side issues of Church life? What of our social justice when some live in luxury whilst others live in poverty in the inner cities, in Third World or war-torn countries? In some places the poor are often too poor or deprived to know how poor they are or to help themselves... Each of us is responsible for the way we as a nation react to social and industrial problems, our neighbours, pollution, poverty, the Third World. Only as we ask in faith can these things be changed.

(b)   This parable has a similar message. Despite all the special care and attention given to this tree, it had invited disaster by not fruiting after three years, nor after a further trial period... God wants us, like Israel, to respond to His Love and He gives us many chances, yet in the long run He does require something back – our love which can only be expressed in sincerity of action. Privilege demands responsibility. Therefore let us not abuse our chances.

(c)   In this parable of the fig tree putting forth its leaves Jesus was saying that neither physical events, nor the ruthlessness and greed of the unscrupulous, even violent, can overthrow the Kingdom of God, whether it be the fall of Jerusalem, Hiroshima, nuclear warfare or revolution. Such events are the sufferings that are to precede the coming of the Kingdom (3) – the end time is approaching. Summer in the Old Testament was a symbol for the Day of the Lord, often seen as a Day of Judgment. (4) Christians, however, have nothing to fear if there has been secret growth leading to fruit bearing, for then they will be able to withstand violence and destruction.

Lord, we see that love is not a passive affair, but demands that same costly love to You and Your family as You showed to us by going to the gallows for us.

To think through:

i.   What is the common theme in these stories about fig trees?

ii.   To whom did Jesus address these words and why? How do these words apply today to us as a nation and individually? Do protests play a role in seeking change or are they the actions of an irresponsible group?

iii.   Who has the right of entry into the Kingdom?

(1)   See Matthew 3 vv 7-12; Luke 3 vv 7-17.

(2)   See Matthew 23 vv 27-28.

(3)   See Matthew 24 vv 4-8.

(4)   See Amos 5 vv 18-24; 8 vv 1-12; et al.

V   THE DEMANDS OF THE KINGDOM II: BE PREPARED OR
ELSE!

INTRODUCTION

The demands that the Kingdom makes on disciples to change, in the power of the Holy Spirit, must be accompanied by a time of secret growth. At the same time there is the further demand to be prepared, like scouts, for the Gospel message is always for the NOW. We must never procrastinate lest the Kingdom in its fulness at the end of the Age comes while we are caught cat-napping.

* * * * * * *

1.   OF SERVANTS WATCHING, AND WAITING AT TABLE

(a) Of Servants Watching For Their Master's Return (Mark 13 vv 32-37; Matthew 24 vv 32-51; Luke 12 vv 35-48).

(b) Of Servants Waiting at Table (Luke 17 vv 7-10).

"It will be good for those servants whose master finds them ready when he comes" (Luke 12 v 37).

* * * * * * *

Many of us will have read books about, or watched programmes on, life in Victorian days, where the servants were portrayed. In a well ordered household each person knew his or her station, from the steward to the lowliest servant. Under the eagle eye of the chief steward who was in the employ of his master there would be security and dignity in working for a good employer. Such a station, nevertheless, required obedience, efficiency and readiness for any situation.

It was precisely these qualities that Jesus culled from the situation of slaves and servants in well-ordered, efficient households in His own day. Although Jesus told His disciples they were no longer servants but friends, (1) yet even as friends with regard to working for the Kingdom they and we must work like slaves. No one can know all God's inmost Sovereign mind and will, especially in connection with the timing of the end of the Age. Disciples must therefore be obedient and efficient as servants, following the example of Jesus, the Suffering Servant, in the Kingdom. We are to be alert and ready for action, like slaves who would tuck their long clothes up for work. Our lamps are to be trimmed with oil – the anointing of the Holy Spirit – and the Word of God should be at our fingertips. We are to be ready to deal with evil marauders into the Kingdom and men of violence, by guarding the Faith and keeping them at bay through prayer and Scripture. And we must be ready to proclaim the Good News of the Kingdom and the return of the Lord at an unknown hour.

Christians are also stewards. Like Ezekiel's watchman, we are responsible not only for our own lives, but also for warning other people of dangers, (2) and proclaiming the Good News that Jesus will save each and everyone from evil and their own folly and ignorance if they will let Him. An urgent message in view of the unknown hour of the end time. This is the responsibility of evangelists, ministers, preachers, priests and yes, all lay Christians exercising their Royal Priesthood, (3) declaring God's praises for mercies received. (3) If we know God's will in these matters, then the very least return we can make for His cancelling our debt to Him through Jesus is to work wholeheartedly for Him, even suffering for Him. Reward enough, but the promise is Eternal Life. (4) If, however, we knowingly fail to pass on the message, then we neglect God's work to our peril and we can only expect to be disciplined. Much is required from those to whom much is given. Privilege and responsibility go together. (5)

As stewards we are also accountable for our own lives and those we are involved with. (5) Our very lives – time, energy, money and talents, our family life – are all to be used sacrificially for His Kingdom. Maybe as Christians we don't squander our money or indulge in pornography, yet our thoughtless enjoyment and spendthrift attitude is at the expense of our less fortunate brothers and sisters in other parts of the world. Our thoughtless attitude to social justice, the conservation of our planet and the ozone layer is a careless misuse of God's Creation.

We must ever remain diligent. Whatever events are happening around us, (6) we can never know when the Lord may be "at the door"(6). It is fatal to procrastinate, thinking that we have plenty of time to prepare, thus pushing God aside from our lives. The message is "TODAY, if you hear his Voice, do not harden your hearts." (7) Tomorrow may be too late. Then "There will be weeping and gnashing of teeth." (8) But the blessed reward for diligence is to be waited on by the Lord Himself at the Great Wedding Feast. (9)

Read and compare meditatively Genesis 1 vv 28-30; Genesis 9 vv 1-7 and Luke 12 v 48, and end by making a prayer out of God's word.

To think through:

i.   What are the characteristics of a servant that God wants to see reproduced in His disciples? Of what importance are they?

ii. What is the difference between a servant and a friend, according to Jesus?

iii. What is a Christian's task (a) as a steward (b) as a watchman? How can these situations be fulfilled?

(1)   See John 13 vv 12-17; 15 vv 14 and 15.
(2)   See Ezekiel 3 vv 17-19; 33 vv 1-20; Romans 12 v 8.
(3)   See Exodus 19 vv 5 and 6; I Peter 2 vv 9 and 10.
(4)   See Matthew 7 v 21.
(5)   See also Genesis 1 vv 28-30, and 2v15.
(6)   See Matthew 24 vv 6-8; Mark 13 vv 7, 8 and 29; Luke 21 vv 9-11 and 31.
(7)   Psalm 95 vv 7 and 8; Hebrews 3 vv 7 and 8.
(8)   Matthew 25 v 30.
(9)   See Revelation 19 v 7.

2.   THE RICH FOOL

(Luke 12 vv 13-21.)

"The ground of a certain rich man produced a good crop. He thought to himself…'Take life easy; eat, drink and be merry.'" But God said to him "You fool! This very night your life will be demanded from you. Then who will get what you have prepared for yourself?" (verses 16, 19b, 20).

* * * * * * *

How glad a farmer is to see his barns full to bursting at the end of a harvest, especially in a country with a variable climate like ours. There is a feeling of having worked in harmony with Nature, of a job well done, of sufficiency for another year, of being blessed by the Creator.

Indeed the Jews believed they were blessed by God if they received material prosperity, (1) a fact that the Rich Fool probably took for granted. In reality he was self-indulgent, greedy and covetous, like the young man who wanted Jesus to endorse his legal claims to property. (2) Rather, Jesus showed him what happens to the greedy and covetous.

One cannot help feeling that Jesus had the story of Joseph in mind. Here was a man who saw that God had provided Egypt with corn enough for seven years. His prudence meant that all who came from Egypt and the surrounding countries were saved from starvation.(3)

Admittedly the Rich Fool stored his grain, too, but there were several vital differences, which could equally well apply to many of us today:-

(a)   He failed to acknowledge the Source of his supplies… How often do we acknowledge the Source of all our supplies? We need to remember that "Everything in heaven and earth is yours." (4) The crops are blessed by God with sun and rain and crowned with His bounty.(5) The Jewish Laws concerning offerings of first-fruits and their Harvest Thanksgivings (6) show us how important is the principle of giving back a portion of what we have been given, in grateful thanks for God to bless further as He chooses and sees the need. "Whoever sows generously will also reap generously." (7) The Rich Man neither thanked his bountiful Creator nor saw beyond himself to those in need. (8)

(b)   This Rich Fool assumed that all his possessions were his by right, yet God gave them as trust for himself and others…(9) It's so easy to think that the Creator's gifts are ours by right and that we are favoured or better if we have more of earth's goodies for one reason or another. Yet all the more responsibility to share. Someone may well say "I worked for it, it's mine!" But the sugar plantation slaves worked hard – for what? Nomads, tribespeople, and many Third World workers work hard to eke out a meagre existence which is snatched from them by unscrupulous, greedy Governments – and we can find other examples in the world of today.

(c)   This man was so pleased with his success that he improved his buildings and dissipated his life in an excess of food, drink and pleasure… Society today, like Esau, wants its birthright now and will do anything to get it for a kind of 'Utopia' with luxury goods. Whatever the Joneses have "they" must have (often incurring enormous debts) and better conditions without putting the effort required into getting them. Esau later learned that, having sold his birthright, there was nothing left for him. Let us learn from Esau before it is too late and turn in repentance from our own indulgences – over-eating, drinking, smoking, fine clothes, even frittering away our time on useless pleasures. Indulgence in the affluent West has brought about an unpleasant economic downturn.

(d)   Alas, there was no thought for the spiritual dimension involving himself or his Maker. Perhaps he was a Sadducee who did not believe in the after-life. God's Love and goodness fell on deaf ears, blind eyes and a closed heart and He entered his life like a thief in the night, (10) finding him totally unprepared for His Love and the great Wedding Feast.

Lord, grant that we may not neglect that part of our beings that relates to You – our spirits. We do so at our peril and so we ask Your Holy Spirit to pervade our lives and turn our minds to You Who are "the ground of our being". (11)

To think through:

i.   What mistake was the Rich Fool making?

ii. There are Christians today who believe that God gives material blessings to His faithful or that such come as a result of faith. Do you agree with this? If so, why? If not, why not?

iii. What, according to Jesus, is the difference between a wise person and a foolish one?

(1)   See Psalm 65 vv 9-13; Amos 9 vv 13-15.
(2)   See Luke 12 vv 13-15.
(3)   See Genesis 41.
(4)   I Chronicles 29 v 11.
(5)   See Psalm 65 vv 9-13.
(6)   See Leviticus 23 vv 22-25; 33-36; 39-43.
(7)   II Corinthians 9 v 6.
(8)   See Deuteronomy 24 vv 19-22.
(9)   See Genesis 1 vv 26-31.
(10) See Matthew 24 v 43; Luke 12 v 39.
(11) From St. Augustine.

1. THE RICH MAN (DIVES) AND LAZARUS

(Luke 16 vv 19-31.)

There was a rich man who was dressed in purple and fine linen and lived in luxury every day. At his gate (1) was laid a beggar named Lazarus, covered with sores and longing to eat what fell from the rich man's table (verses 19-21).

* * * * * * *

Rich man, Poor man. This parable reads like a modern television documentary on affluence versus abject poverty. (2) The scene could be Britain with its great divide, the affluent West versus the Third World, or unscrupulous, wealthy Governments versus the poorest of the poor.

Yes, these two men were the total opposite of each other. The very anonymity of their names is intended to typify the section of society each comes from, both in Jesus' time and ours...

The World

'RICH MAN' (in Latin 'Dives'),never noticed or did anything for "Poor Man",for he held such people in contempt . Today many affluent are callous and indifferent.

'POOR MAN' or Lazarus- 'God is my help'.His only gratuity came from 'Rich Man's scraps .Today,we offer scraps of mercy out of our purses.

'Rich Man' was rich by whatever means. He obviously believed that all his wealth was his by right. Today,many cling tenaciously to this belief.

'Poor Man' was poor for whatever reason. A beggar was,alas for his status,beyond hope of salvation. Today,nearly two thirds of the world's despised are poor through no fault of their own.

'Rich Man' was attired in finest purple cloth only afforded by the very rich. Today,many afford luxuries and fine clothes at the expense of the poor.

IN THE PARABLE

'Rich Man' never gave this a thought

BOTH ARE CHILDREN OF GOD

'Poor Man' had no inhibition about receiving gratuity.

'Poor Man' was dressed in rags. Today,the outcasts and refugees are still in rags or cast-off clothes from charity shops,or Christian and Oxfam parcels.

'Rich Man' was embalmed with expensive unguents. Today,many spend a fortune on cosmetics and perfume.

'Poor Man' was covered with sores and smelled. Today,there are many adults and small children with sores and distended stomachs. 'Rich Man' licks his wounds with a few pennies.

'Rich Man' feeds daily on sumptuous food. Today,the affluent eat the goods from 'Poor Man's countries,paying ridiculously low money for his efforts.

'Poor Man' may only eat two or three times a week. Lazarus lived off scraps thrown carelessly from 'Rich Mans' table. Today,few meals of any nutritional value are available to those in third world communities.

'Rich Man',if he thought at all,believed God had blessed him by giving him material goods and they were his. Today,this principle often still holds good.

'Poor Man' knew his poverty and destitution and he could only cling to indiscriminate scraps from his benefactor. Today,some are too poor to know that they are poor.

The scene shifts. Both men die. What is depicted in the next world finds an echo today.

100

LIFE AFTER DEATH

Heaven   Hell

'POOR MAN' has a common burial. He is still a child of God	G	'RICH MAN' died with all the trimmings. He is still a child of God.
'Poor Man' finds relief close to Abraham and Jesus.	U	'Rich Man' is perhaps surprised to find there is an after life (a Sadducee?).
'Poor Man' is comforted. God has helped him out of anguish.	L F	'Rich Man' in hell is in torment in the fiery furnace of his own punishment.
'Poor Man' receives God's gratuities. His earthly poverty is reversed in spiritual blessings (v.25)	F I	'Rich Man' was told that he had received all the good things in the world whilst he was alive.
'Poor Man' had found the burden imposed by "religion" too great.	X E D	'Rich Man' and his brothers have been warned against evil by the prophets.
'Poor Man' having no expectations,could more easily accept Jesus.		'Rich Man' refused to listen to the prophets and will refuse to hear the Risen Christ.

Again, as in this world, Jesus knew that things were little different regarding the next world!

Lord, the great divide between a few rich and many poor grows.
Help us as Your disciples to feel the sufferings of the poor.
Let us never grow callous, uncaring or just not noticing.
Forgive our sins of omission in this matter and give us thankful hearts for what we have.

To think through:

i.   How did the Rich Man go wrong? What was his sin?

ii.   What expectations can the poor have (a) in this life and (b) in the next world?

iii.   What can and will you do about your findings?

(1)   See Deuteronomy 15 vv 1-11.
(2)   See 1 Samuel 2 vv 4 and 5; Luke 1 vv 52 and 53.

4.   THE WISE AND FOOLISH VIRGINS

(Matthew 25 vv 1-13.)

"Afterward the other maidens came also, saying 'Lord, Lord, open to us.' But he replied, 'Truly, I say to you, I do not know you'" (verse 11) (Revised Standard Version).

* * * * * * *

Those of us who have been late for a performance, and found the doors closed against us, will know the bitter disappointment of missing the performance, or part of it. That's how the five foolish virgins must have felt when they found the door shut in their faces. And who in their senses would miss the joy and honour of being in attendance on the bride and welcoming the bridegroom when he appeared?

The five wise virgins were not, as at first sight might appear, being selfish in keeping the spare oil that they would have brought for themselves. No, they had responded to a personal invitation and had prepared themselves for the occasion prudently, especially as the exact moment that the bridegroom would appear was not known till almost the time. The five foolish virgins had received the same personal invitation, yet in the time following they had been indolent and not bothered to prepare properly. Worse, they were even prepared to borrow and lean on other people's resources to get into the wedding when they could well have been prepared. They were left outside through their own stupidity.

Once again we see Jesus representing Himself as the Bridegroom and the two types of virgins as two types of people. Jesus came to earth to issue an Invitation to everyone to accept Salvation and to attend His Wedding Feast at the end of the Age. He issues the Invitation more than once, till at length the coming of the Bridegroom is announced, and that is a very rapid process. He and the final consummation of the Kingdom are "near, right at the door". (1) So those who hear and receive the Invitation initially have time in which to prepare. The only right of entry to the Feast is by personal response and readiness to accept such a unique Invitation to an individual – outwardly and inwardly. Outward response often occurs in a service of Dedication, Baptism, Confirmation, or Baptism in the Spirit. The oil in the lamps and the spare oil is the anointing of the Holy Spirit and the daily infilling of His Presence, maintained through inward response, secret growth and preparation. A personal relationship and communication with God is developed by prayer and meditation, and by asking for and using the gifts and fruit of the Spirit. No-one else can respond for an individual. Even the Baptism vows, undertaken by Godparents for an infant, have to be completed and accepted personally later. And no-one may borrow or lean on anyone else's spiritual resources. The uniqueness of the Invitation to each individual suggests the importance of the occasion, and something not to be missed.

Surely it is worth the simple effort required to appropriate this urgent message and act on it lest the Bridegroom comes suddenly and we find the door is closed with an air of finality and seemingly no more chances. Is it too late then? Who knows but God in His mercy. Yet we are told that the unfulfilled tasks of the foolish virgins are rewarded by their being cast out, wailing and yelping like dogs outside a closed door. The readiness of the wise virgins, however, whatever they are doing, will bring the happiness of rejoicing with the Bridegroom and His friends.

Give me oil in my lamp, keep me burning.

Give me oil in my lamp, I pray.

Give me oil in my lamp, keep me burning,

Keep me burning to the end of day.

Sing Hosanna, sing Hosanna, sing Hosanna to the King of Kings.

Sing Hosanna, sing Hosanna, sing Hosanna to the King. (2)

To think through:

i.   Why do you think that God does not tell us the exact hour when Jesus, the Bridegroom, will return?

ii.   Are there any signs that we can look for as to when to expect His return, even if not the exact time? If so, what are these signs? (See Mark 13.)

iii.   If, as we know Him to be, a God of Love, why does He lay such importance on acceptance and readiness?

(1)   Matthew 24 v 33.
(2)   From "Give Me Joy in My Heart " v 4 in Hymns Old and New – New Anglican Edition Traditional-arranged Kevin Mayhew 1996.

5.   THE GREAT SUPPER (1)

(Luke 14 vv 12-24.)

"Come, for everything is now ready. But they all alike began to make excuses" (verses 17 and 18).

* * * * * * *

If you have ever given a dinner party and found your guests dropping out one by one, you begin to feel disappointed, then angry because your invitation, with all it has to offer, is being rejected as well as you yourself. How much worse when it is God Whose Invitation is being rejected and how disappointed He is that His loving offer is cast aside.

We have already noted (2) how Jesus urged His host to invite all the lowly people, the downtrodden and outcasts he could find when entertaining. This would bring more blessing in Heaven than inviting those who could repay him. One guest, on hearing mention of the Age of the Resurrection, ejaculated how blessed were those who were privileged to eat at the great Wedding Feast. (3) The righteous, Law-abiding Jews believed God was preparing such for them to the exclusion of tax-collectors and sinners – those who were totally unable to keep the rigid Law – and indeed Gentiles.

Jesus had a shock coming for this man, as for all Pharisees and Sadducees who believed they were privileged before God. Those who had received the original invitation in this parable excused themselves when it came to the actual day. Their excuses looked genuine enough with their new businesses, farming enterprises or domestic affairs. (4) The point was that these people had already accepted the original Invitation and were waiting for the actual timing, so they had no excuse and indeed were insulting their host by opting out. Jesus' hearers would recognise that He was referring to them. Those who believed that their very election as Jews earned them a place at the Feast would be shocked to discover that because of their callous attitude the situation was reversed and their places would be taken, when urged to, by the very people they despised and failed to help.

So it is today. There is the Invitation – "Come to me." (5) Yet there are those who allow business claims, new toys and possessions, or married life to crowd God out, leaving no time for worship or helping others. All these things have their place but without God they lose His blessing on the very things they consider important, as well as fellowship within the family of God. Or again, we want our church services, our feasts, our music and dancing to ourselves. We associate only with those we like, rather than the tiresome little old lady who is dying, the ex-prisoner, shop-lifter, drug addict or dosser. And we exclude many from Christianity by presenting a false image of Christ. We are shocked by the unconventional, and so exclude ourselves from the blessings of God…

Yes we, too, like the Jews so often have our shutters up, existing in our own little world, and we present our excuses – Sunday trading, business and domestic affairs, thus excluding God and His little ones and organising our own lives. We are judging ourselves and then on that day we may be shocked to find ourselves excluded from the Feast and our places taken by the poor, the drop-outs and those we despise and find unlovely, yet who recognise their need and thus eagerly accept the Invitation.

Lord, grant that we may put all our exclusiveness and excuses for not doing Your Will aside and learn to love Your needy sons and daughters..

To think through:

i.   What lessons shall we, as disciples, take from this parable?
ii. Why could it be easy for Christians to fall into the same mistake as the Pharisees? What action could be taken to avoid this?

iii.   What excuses might Christians present to the Lord for not accepting His Invitation?

(1)   Authorised Version; ("Banquet" in New International Version).
(2)   See "Humility" – III, 2.
(3)   See Isaiah 25 vv 6-10.
(4)   See Deuteronomy 24 v 5.
(5)   Matthew 11 v 28.

6.   THE MARRIAGE OF THE KING'S SON

(Matthew 22 vv 1-14.)

"A king…prepared a wedding banquet for his son. He sent his servants to those who had been invited…but they refused to come. Then he sent some more servants, and said…'Tell those who have been invited that I have prepared my dinner… Come to the wedding banquet.' But they paid no attention… 'those I invited did not deserve to come' "(verses 2, 3, 4, 5, 8).

* * * * * * *

Here is a parable in two acts, similar to, yet different from the Great Supper. The first act contains the original invitations to the guests and their excuses, the host's anger, rejection and casting out of those guests, and the forceful allusion to the burning of their city. The second act concerns the issuing of new invitations to those who could not have expected such an invitation.

In the first act, once again, those who received the first invitations had plenty of time to prepare and arrange to be free when the call should come. Yet those guests just assumed their places were guaranteed, despite their unpreparedness and continued excuses. Jesus saw that God's message and messengers, the Prophets, had already been rejected, even killed, as He, too, would be, His disciples living to see the prophesied destruction of the Holy City, (1) Jerusalem, in A.D. 70.

The curtain falls on Act I but only in the same instant to rise on Act II. The drama shifts from the privileged who should have inherited the Kingdom to those out on the street corners. The King ordered that his gratuitous invitation should be offered to all and sundry, and as suggested earlier, even those undeserving and unworthy people who would otherwise have no expectancy of such, with the opportunity for changing to fine linen clothes, (2) or righteous deeds. Yet, even after the opportunity afforded by the time for preparation, one guest entered totally unchanged, in his rags and not in the wedding garment provided. He simply had made no effort.

This parable speaks to us today much as in Jesus' day. God still issues His Invitation and asks us to prepare for the Wedding Feast in the ultimate fulfilment of the Kingdom. We acknowledge His call but are we prepared to live by His Word? Rather we accept Christianity on our own terms and crucify the Lord all over again, and the messengers of His Good News, like Martin Luther King (3a) or Archbishop Janani Luwum. (3b) Perhaps we need it said to us again that we should not assume that just being a Christian and saying "Lord, Lord" (4) will get us to the Wedding Feast. Rather, if we have encountered His Love, we will want to seek His will in Scripture and by prayer, and do it. And what is His will but to love God and our neighbours? Love has to be expressed in action for how can we say we love God if we do not help our neighbours? (5) Else those who are around on our street corners, those who have lost their dignity and self-respect through drink, drugs, crime, sex, glue-sniffing may well take our place. Many of these accept, if they hear, having nothing to lose, yet even so change is required in them just as it was for Zacchaeus, (6) and which thus brought about his salvation.

Lord, help us to change and be prepared for Your Feast.

To think through:

i.   Who are the people to whom Jesus issues His Invitation (a) in His own day (b) today? Does this surprise us? Do we see ourselves included in this Invitation?

ii.   How do you interpret the wedding garment and Jesus' Righteousness? What does it mean to put on His Righteousness and how can we do it? (See Revelation 19 vv 7-8.)

iii. What terms and limitations do we set on our entry to the Kingdom?

(1)   See Matthew 24 vv 1-2, 14-20; Mark 13 vv 1-4, 14-20; Luke 21 vv 1-7, 20-24.

(2)   See Revelation 19 v 8.

(3a)   American Civil Rights leader murdered 1968.

(3b)   Archbishop of Uganda murdered 1976.

(4)   Matthew 7 v 21.

(5)   See I John 2 vv 9-10; James 1 vv 26-27.

(6)   See Luke 19 vv 1-10.

7.   THE WEDDING FEAST PROPHESIED: TO BE ENJOYED

BY "PEOPLE FROM EAST AND WEST, AND FROM NORTH

AND SOUTH"

(Luke 13 vv 22-30, Matthew 8 vv 5-13)

"There will be weeping there and gnashing of teeth when you see…
yourselves thrown out. People will come from east and west and north
and south and will take their places at the feast in the kingdom of God"
(Luke 13 vv 28-29).

* * * * * * *

Today the boundaries of our world have become very much smaller,
so that it has been described as a global village. So, in these days of
communication and the mingling of East and West, North and South, all
races, colours and creeds, these words of Jesus seem less revolutionary
than they would have done when first spoken. Nevertheless the message
is still crystal clear and the meaning as pungent as ever.

Matthew and Luke have received these words of Jesus in different
contexts, but clearly with the same warning in mind. In Matthew the
words illustrate the absolute faith of a Gentile Centurion who was
himself under authority and expected both to obey and be obeyed.
Likewise he believed that the authority of Jesus' Word would be
obeyed. It was belief such as this that would gain a person entrance
to the Kingdom and not the assumption that being one of the Chosen
Race would ensure entry. So here Jesus foreshadows the inclusion
of Gentiles, as well as Jews, whose hearts are circumcised and not
necessarily their bodies. (1) In Luke these words came as the climax
to similar teaching – to enter the Kingdom by the narrow door – or
gate (2) of acceptance of the Lord's grace and favour, followed by
doing His Will. Election necessitates good, not iniquitous works. (3)

Jesus was restricted by time, energy and space and therefore
concentrated His teaching on the Jews, who, through the Holy Spirit's

influence, would later be led to fan out to the Gentiles. Yet we can be glad that He gave such clear pointers to the inclusion of Gentiles into His Kingdom, both in these words, in parables like the Great Supper (4) and the Marriage of the King's Son, (5) in the breaking down of the "dividing wall of hostility", (6) and the wall in the Temple courtyard which barred Gentiles from entering the Temple itself, on pain of death. (6)

These words need to be said to us again today. Often, even unintentionally, we put up barriers, expect other Christians to worship in the same way as us, and we may feel quite strange in the presence of African or South American Christians who are far more liberated than we are. What counts is not so much the expression of worship as their prayer and praise and the gifts and fruit of the Spirit in the growth of churches. Baptism is a very real experience. Healings seem to happen on a vaster scale than in the West because belief is more simple, trusting and straightforward especially in areas of deprivation and lack of medical assistance. AND they are now sending missionaries to Europe!

I have been privileged in my own life to meet people of many nationalities, colours and creeds – in particular a Buddhist Thailander and a Hindu, both sympathetic to Christianity, from the East; a Lutheran American, from the West; a Russian Orthodox, from the North; an Aboriginal Episcopalian Australian and a Roman Catholic Ugandan Asian, from the South. Each one taught me about coinherence in Christ and the reality of people serving Christ in one another, caring for the poor and lost. Each was an example of simple goodness and holiness, proving Jesus' words over and over again. And there are others who serve God and their fellow humans in their own way, having never heard the Good News. These, I believe, God will deal with mercifully according to their understanding and application of the Universal Law of justice and mercy. We are indeed in for some surprises at the Wedding Feast.

Lord, let us learn again the lesson You are teaching us, that our entry into the Kingdom depends on our attitudes.

To think through:

i.   Are the ways in which Matthew and Luke have presented this prophecy contradictory or complementary?

ii.   Do these words seem revolutionary today or have they lost their significance for Christians?

iii.   What is God looking for in those who accept His Invitation and why?

(1)   See Deuteronomy 10 v 16; Acts 7 v 51.
(2)   See also Matthew 7 v 13.
(3)   See Mark 7 vv 14-23; Matthew 25 vv 31-45; et al.
(4)   See Luke 14 vv 12-24.
(5)   See Matthew 22 vv 1-14.
(6)   Ephesians 2 v 14.

A   THE MYSTERY OF THE KINGDOM UNFOLDS

INTRODUCTION

The tantalising bait of a prize with an enormous sum of money at Wimbledon is enough to make every competitor train with no slacking so as to be fit and ready. How much more will we want to be ready for the greatest prize of all – the gift of Eternal Life. The necessity for such readiness is enhanced when we begin to understand the reversionary principles of the Kingdom over against the world's standards.

1.   SIMON THE PHARISEE

(Luke 7 vv 36-50.)

Jesus said to Simon " You did not give me water for my feet... You did not give me a kiss...You did not put oil on my head" (vv 40, 44, 45 and 47).

* * * * * * *

As we peer in on this little dinner party held in Jesus' honour we see the unfolding of the Divine drama wherein Jesus acted out the forgiving Love of God in human flesh. Everyone who came into contact with that radiating Love was given the opportunity to receive it as well as forgiveness and be changed. The two people who came under the Divine searchlight there were themselves unconsciously acting out a part, too, but they received that Love differently according to their own situations. Both Simon, a Pharisee, and the woman were re-enacting Adam and Eve – "Man's" – fall from Grace.

Sadly Simon had neglected the three social duties of a host – the welcoming kiss, the foot washing and anointing with oil when Jesus arrived at his house – a sign of disrespect and negligence, especially in a hot and dusty country. Many people, like Simon, seem curious to encounter Jesus, even to make overtures, but never become properly 'engaged'. They want the perks of a feast but without allowing themselves to be changed. Entertaining Christ means getting oneself involved in the 'feast of humanity' – the grime of life as indeed many do. It involves bestowing a warming "kiss of love" on those in distress; "washing the feet" of those unable to help themselves; and offering "the oil of anointing" and comfort to the homeless on our streets, the sick, those in prison, the dying. We, like the Jews, know such facts well, yet often disregard them. (1) Why?

The answer is that many, even good Christians, feel self-sufficient and that they can manage without God. Like Simon they believe that they do little wrong. I've heard people say, "I'm not a bad person. I don't commit adultery, steal or kill. I don't need God to run my life", thus contrasting themselves with those who do such things, much as Simon did silently from his secure home. Yet even the most Pharisaic amongst us would recognise that only God is Righteous (2) and not all the fulfilling of the Law can make anyone righteous. For people to believe that they are good means theirs is the greater sin in not recognising their short-fall from God's Righteousness, (3) which the Prophets spelled out in terms of love and justice (4) to one's, often poorer, neighbours, much as the Deuteronomist did. (5) How can anyone believe he or she is righteous on their own merits whilst fellow humans are poor or homeless?

Such curiosity, which nevertheless lacks resulting action, self righteousness and the failure to be aware of one's need for God, or one's sinfulness, are patronising and condescending to Him. So, too, such hearts are closed to God's overflowing, forgiving Love.

We find an echo today of the woman's apparent self-indulgence, and cravings for 'sex'. Many cannot wait to be married, or simply live together. Or circumstances have led them to the streets and so they turn to the unsatisfying, passing love of another human for comfort, money or whatever, rather than God's liberating Love. Many also find Christianity's often Pharisaic attitude too harsh and exclusive for them, yet when faced with the reality of God and Jesus they have no axes to grind. Those who, like this woman, or 'Bess', one of today's

116

'lost causes', come looking for scraps of Divine mercy in humans, recognise the hopelessness of their situation. Yet they find their deep inner (spiritual) needs are met when God pours out His Love to them, either through a personal encounter with them or the loving actions of some human being. Then they are able to receive of God's bountiful Love and forgiveness. So we see criminals and drug addicts today come, much as the woman did, giving their costliest treasures – themselves – to the Lord.

Lord, help us to understand ourselves clearly and to realise that we can only be right in Your sight through Your generosity in allowing Jesus to die on our behalf.

To think through:

i.   What kind of person was (a) Simon (b) the woman? What groups of people do they represent?
ii.   What does this story say to each of us?
iii.   For whom is God's grace and forgiveness?

(1)   See Matthew 25 vv 31-46.
(2)   See Mark 2 vv 1-12; Romans 1 v 17; et al.
(3)   See Romans 3 v 23.
(4)   See Amos 5 vv 18-24; Isaiah 1; et al.
(5)   See Deuteronomy 15 vv 7, 8 and 11; 24 v 17.

2.   THE LABOURERS IN THE VINEYARD

(Matthew 20 vv 1-16.)

"The kingdom of heaven is like a landowner who went out early in the morning to hire men to work in his vineyard. He agreed to pay them a denarius for the day and sent them into his vineyard. About the third… sixth…ninth…and the eleventh hour…he said to them: 'You also go and work in my vineyard..' When evening came…those came who were hired first …expected to receive more! But each one of them also received a denarius" (verses 1-9).

* * * * * * *

How demoralising it is to wait in an unemployment queue only to find that those who came later, or even last, got a job before you or were to be paid as much as or more than yourself. It's certainly unjust looked at in worldly terms, as journeymen, or men hired on a precarious daily basis in harvest-time in Jesus' days would well know, their wages depending on the whims of their employer.

Not so the employer in Jesus' parable. He employed the first men at 6 a.m., agreeing a contract of a denarius (1) – a penny? – for a day's work. To the others whom he employed throughout the day he said he would give what was right or fair. When they were all gathered up they received their pay in reverse order, those coming at the eleventh hour likewise getting a denarius. Those who had entered earlier into their employer's contract felt that they should have received more, but they forgot they had entered into a contract and this employer kept his word as a man of integrity and far surpassed the bounds of generosity, necessity and justice.

In Old Testament times a Vineyard represented Israel (2) and Jesus took over this image. The original labourers represented the Jewish nation who broke the Covenant. In the New Israel it was to be those who accepted God's free gift who would receive Eternal Life, (3) not those Jews who sat on their privileges expecting to inherit the Kingdom by right of birth and election.

Jesus' message holds good for us as for the Pharisees to whom He spoke. Just as they were annoyed with Jesus for being generous towards those who were sinners, so we see some who want to keep the privilege of serving God to themselves and wanting the best positions in the church. They cannot accept younger or newer, even Spirit-filled Christians taking a lead in their stead. And if they have served God over a long period, then they expect a bigger share of the reward. Yet God made a contract, or agreement, with every Christian in Baptism or Dedication, much as He had with the Jews. And that agreement was Eternal life for those who believe in and accept Jesus as Saviour. Nothing was said about length of service, nor our own merits. Rather Eternal Life is a free gift, (3) which nevertheless depends on the attitude of the recipient to one's fellow humans for such a bounty. (4)

Quite clearly Jesus is saying that it is not privilege, but willingness to embrace change and to accept and serve our fellow humans that counts. This gives God the opportunity to put people in contact with His Love, and at the same time it gives us the opportunity to show our love for Him and His children. He sees all men and women as equal, therefore all must receive the same chance and the same wage.

Perhaps it should be said again that no-one deserves Eternal life on his or her own merits – only through Jesus Christ can one receive such a gift. God makes it plain that those who remain faithful to His Commandments in the Spirit of love will inherit the Kingdom. Entry to the Kingdom is seen to be revolutionary and reversionary.

Lord, how often have we grumbled and been guilty of not living up to the privilege of being members of Your Kingdom... Teach us to love and serve You knowing that we already enjoy the blessings of the Kingdom and to rejoice when others receive those blessings too.

To think through:

i.   What reversionary principles are involved in this story?

ii.   To what extent is the privilege of (a) living in reasonably affluent Britain and (b) being a Christian important to each of us? What responsibilities does privilege bring?

iii.   Is Eternal Life within the grasp of everyone who is born?

(1)   A denarius was a day's wage for a labourer in Jesus' time.
(2)   See Isaiah 5 vv 1-7.
(3)   See Romans 5 vv 15-21.
(4)   See Galatians 5 vv 13-36.

3. "I AM THE WAY AND THE TRUTH AND THE LIFE"

(John 14 vv 1-9.)

Jesus said, "I AM the way and the truth and the life. No-one comes to the Father except through me" (verse 6).

* * * * * * *

I remember once seeing on a former television series called "The Goodies" a sign depicting the old maxim "All roads lead to Rome", placed on the seashore of the English Channel, with "ROME" signed in every direction. Imagine the fun The Goodies had trying to decide which way to take!

Many people likewise believe that "All roads lead to God." This belief, however, could take us along many devious, even false routes. But the Way of Jesus leads to the fulfilment of life by trusting in the Truth, (1) and plenitude of Divine Life and Love. (2) The only true and ultimate loving revelation of God is Jesus Christ, the Son of God, (3) through Whom alone comes the gift of Salvation. (4) In the long run, either here, or in the life hereafter, before being confronted with the total reality of God, we shall need to accept Salvation through Jesus, whatever our beliefs. This is not to deny faith genuinely held by those of other Religions but rather that Christians can enter into dialogue with them and show by example that Christ is All in All without preaching at them.

"I AM THE WAY. " Early Christians were known as people, or followers, of the Way. (5) Many had seen, known and touched Jesus during His Life and Ministry, even been His disciples or Apostles (6) and learnt, even as we, too, are learning what that Way is. It is the response of love to Love. However, this way of love does not take us through a bed of roses, but is rather a way of denial, of servitude and suffering – even of being crucified, (7) metaphorically or literally, as some have been in warfare and strife. This world's standards are seen to be turned upside down... There is a poster showing people of all sorts and of all nationalities gazing upwards at a Cross on a hill – Yes, The Cross of Jesus. It draws and compels, demanding a response.

"I AM THE TRUTH. " John aptly describes Jesus as "full of grace and truth". (8) Our God is a gracious God, showing us the meaning of Truth – Reality or Wholeness – by His Love and mercy in caring for all His children. And those who follow Jesus in the Way measure themselves by His yardstick or standards, rather than by the rigidity of the old Law or any set of moral precepts. This TRUTH of God makes us free (9) in conscience, and thus enables us to live Life as He meant us to live it, even if that freedom takes us along paths of opposition and disfavour in doing His Will. Yes, evil has been conquered but God has chosen not to limit human free-will.

"I AM THE LIFE. " Life comes through knowing Jesus Who is Truth. He came to give us Life in abundance (10) – Eternal Life, or that quality of life wherein God's Reign is Sovereign. Jesus, in Whom all the fulness of the Godhead dwells bodily, (11) achieved this by dying and rising to Life. And we, too, may pass through death to be made alive in Him, through the forgiveness of our sins, (12) and by receiving His Heavenly Food.

* * * * * * *

Oh Lord Jesus, You are the Way, Who points us to the Truth which leads to Life.Grant that we may not wander from that Way nor refuse to accept the Truth which sets us free to embrace that Life which brings us into Your Kingdom (13).

To think through:

i.   What would you say to a person of another faith who perhaps believes that all roads lead to God?

ii.   Since it is Christian belief that Salvation can only come through Jesus, what of those who have never heard of the Gospel, or have never heard the message personally?

122

iii.   What does it mean to dialogue with those of other faiths?

(1)   See also John 8 vv 45-46.
(2)   See Ephesians 1; Colossians 1 vv 15-20.
(3)   See John 1 vv 1-18; 5 vv 17-47; 6 vv 25-51; 8 vv 12-58.
(4)   See Acts 4 v 12; cf also John's Gospel.
(5)   See Acts 19 vv 9 and 23; 24 v 14.
(6)   See I John 1 v 1; cf The Gospels.
(7)   See Mark 8 vv 31-38; 10 vv 32-45; et al.
(8)   John 1 vv 14-18.
(9)   See John 8 vv 31-32.
(10) See John 10 v 10.
(11) See Colossians 2 v 9; cf 1 v 19.
(12) See Colossians 2 v 13.
(13) See Matthew 7 v 14 (Authorised Version).

B   A FORETASTE OF THE WEDDING FEAST:

THE MESSIAH REVEALS HIMSELF TO THOSE WHO HAVE

EYES TO SEE AND EARS TO HEAR (1)

INTRODUCTION

Perhaps, above all, the lesson that has emerged over the last three sections is that the principles of Kingdom Life are the reverse of all the ideals that the world holds dear – privilege, money, position, honour and authority. During the rest of this chapter we shall see how Jesus leads us on to discover the Spiritual blessings of the Kingdom.

(1) See Mark 4 vv9 and 12.

* * * * * * *

1.   FROM THE LORD'S PRAYER "GIVE US THIS DAY OUR

DAILY BREAD" (1)

(Matthew 6 vv 9-13; Luke 11 vv 2-4.)

"Our Father in heaven… Give us this day our daily bread" (Matthew 6 vv 9-11). (Authorised Version)

* * * * * * *

The words "Our Father" (1) must mean more to us today than ever before. Television quickly brings us into contact with the joys and sorrows of our brothers and sisters on the other side of the world. It would be a callous person who did not identify with them since all of us are God's children, made in His image. (2) He is Our Father and our Communal Source, Who loves us and knows our needs before we ask. Yet by our asking He is able to touch the spirits and hearts of those who have what we or our neighbours need.

Please will You 'give us' shows our dependence on God Who provides sun and rain, (3) soil, food and minerals – all resources for our needs and those of the world – in abundance. However we have to co-operate with God by harvesting, preparing and sharing out the goods and earnings fairly throughout the world and by sensible stewardship of our planet. (4) This involves conservation, good forestry, no pollution, careful use of energy and goods. We need to take this absolutely seriously if our prayer for daily bread for all God's children is to be answered.

"Give us this day our daily bread" (1) (bread for today and tomorrow) follows Jesus' teaching generally, that we should not worry about provisions beyond the present day but "seek first his kingdom and his righteousness". (5) So we pray for our needs one day at a time, for does not God's provision of sun and rain today, give us our bread (food and other needs) for tomorrow? The Jews would pray in the morning for enough bread for the day and likewise again in the evening for the new day just starting at 6 p.m.!

However, Jesus always deals with the whole person – body, mind and spirit – as He clearly demonstrated in His Temptations – "Man does not live on bread alone, but on every word that comes from the mouth of God." (6) So our daily bread is also our spiritual bread, appropriated as we read Scripture and receive our spiritual sustenance. We shall be the more satisfied when we are at peace with God. Indeed if one "feeds" people with the Good News of Jesus first then they will want to try to improve their material and physical lot (though this Good News badly needs to reach the ears of those Governments who suppress their subjects to keep themselves rich!).

At the Last Supper Jesus took Bread and Wine and transferred them to our use as our spiritual food – His Very Body and Blood. (7) Thus united with Him spiritually we shall want to share all we have, both spiritually and materially, with others, and so finally bring in that Kingdom where Jesus will preside. Our physical bread of today becomes our spiritual Bread of tomorrow at the Eternal Wedding Feast. (8)

*Lord, we are all Your children, yet Your heart must bleed when
You see how greedy many of us are. Bread for the world can
be a reality only as we obey Your Laws. Yet we need Your Holy
Spirit's pervading influence to achieve this. Come Holy Spirit.*

To think through:

i.   What does sensible stewardship involve for Christians?

ii. Do we, as the Church and as individual Christians, really pray
     that Governments may release surplus supplies and that the war
     lords will allow their subjects to be fed?

iii. In what ways can we help to prevent people starving and avert
     drought and famine?

(1) See Luke 11 vv 2 and 11-13.
(2) See Genesis 1 v 26; cf Matthew 5 v 9; Romans 8 vv 16
     and 21; et al.
(3) See Genesis 8 v 22; Psalm 65 vv 9-13; Isaiah 55 vv 10-13.
(4) See Genesis 1 vv 28-31; cf Isaiah 1 vv 10-17; 5 vv 1-23;
     Amos 5 vv 8, 10-24; et al.
(5) Matthew 6 v 33.
(6) Matthew 4 v 4; cf Luke 4 v 4; Deuteronomy 8 v 3.
(7) See Matthew 26 vv 26-29; Mark 14 vv 22-25; Luke 22 vv
     17-20; John 6 vv 25-65.
     I Corinthians 11 vv 23-25.
(8) See Revelation 7 v 17; 19 v 9.

2.   JESUS "THE MESSIAH" FEEDS FIVE THOUSAND

(Matthew 14 vv 13-21; Mark 6 vv 30-34; Luke 9 vv 10-17; John 6 vv

1-15; cf Matthew 15 vv 29-38.)

Taking the five loaves, and the two fish and looking up to heaven, he gave thanks, and broke the loaves. Then he gave them to his disciples to set before the people. He also divided the two fish among them all. They all ate and were satisfied (Mark 6 vv 41-42).

* * * * * * *

Major events like Royal Weddings or disasters receive front page coverage in all the daily newspapers. So, too, this amazing miracle where Jesus fed so many with so little. All four Evangelists have given it space and in-depth coverage.

The events of, and surrounding, this miracle are set in the context of worship. Indeed, all Creation is quite often unwittingly worshipping or moving rhythmically – dancing – sometimes in time and tune with the Creator, sometimes not, according to our mis-use of free-will.

Those who encounter Jesus, the Lord of the Dance, (1) and become disciples, whether during His time on earth, or now, begin to measure their step with His, involving them in a new and harmonious Dance. And each fresh encounter means a change of direction in the Dance along the Way with Him.

Like His principal dancers, the Apostles, Jesus bids us spend some time 'off stage', alone with Him to receive of His grace and to try to measure our step with His again. Yet no sooner do we try to get 'off stage' than the crowds come bursting in upon us from the wings, clamouring that we do something about their problems. Here are sheep without a shepherd, leaderless people throughout the world longing to be led and fed by their Creator, even if they do not 'recognise' Him as such. They even wish Him to act by force to stop violence, just as the Jews wished Jesus to overthrow the Romans.

We want to be alone. "Send them away, Lord", we cry. Yet, just as Jesus bade the Apostles feed the crowds (2) so He bids us to do something for them. "Alas, with what?" we cry out again. There's the same poverty and helplessness of response and ill-measured steps as with the Apostles. Yet Jesus Himself knew what He would do, and what source to tap…

Yes, Jesus blazed the trail for us there in Galilee and set His actions in the timelessness of Covenant worship. (3) He TOOK the bread, gave a Sabbath and Passover BLESSING and THANKSGIVING over it, BROKE it, and GAVE it to His disciples as ministers to share out amongst the crowds. Just as the Israelites were fed in the wilderness in Moses' time, (4) and were satisfied, so, too, they were in Jesus' time – a foreshadowing of the New Covenant inaugurated at the Last Supper. (5) There, Jesus commanded the Apostles to recall His breaking of Bread and sharing of Wine and to appropriate His Body and Blood, broken and poured out for us all on Calvary – Spiritual blessings for themselves and for the whole world. As often as we too recall this once-for-all sacrifice, (6) His Body is broken and His Blood is offered for ourselves, for the crowds and for the world, until Jesus returns to inaugurate and preside at His Wedding Feast. (7)

As we pause in our time alone with Jesus before the Cross, pondering on His Word and breaking Bread at the Eucharist, we are filled anew with the inexhaustible riches and fulness of the Creator. (8) Like Jesus before us, we can now reach out to the crowds who ever break in on us, longing to be freed from hatred, violence, greed, fear, pointless suffering and killings. It is our responsibility and privilege to lift the world and its problems up to the Lord on the Cross, asking Him to redeem each and all from sin, from their agonising suffering, from poverty or even from the wealth that is blind or callous to others' needs.

No, those crowds will not go away. They are our brothers and sisters and they clamour for their Saviour now as they once clamoured for Jesus.

Lord, now we see what a privilege it is to minister to Your little ones when we are close to You in times of refreshment and solitude. It is then that we can most fully reach out to them and place them in Your care.

To think through:

i.   Where are these four actions of taking bread, blessing it, breaking and giving it, to be found in the Christian Church?

ii. What does Jesus want us to do about the crowds?

iii. How important is Holy Communion to us? Why?

(1)   See *The Lord of The Dance*. A. Duncan (Helios 1972).
(2)   See all four accounts.
(3)   See Matthew 26 vv 26-30; Mark 14 vv 22-25; Luke 22 vv 17-20; John 6 vv 25-65.
(4)   See Exodus 16 vv 1-36.
(5)   See VII 6.
(6)   See Hebrews 10 v 14.
(7)   See Revelation 19 vv 7-9.
(8)   See Ephesians 1.

3.   "I AM THE BREAD OF LIFE"

(John 6 vv 25-71.)

"I AM the bread of Life; he who comes to me will never go hungry, and he who believes in me will never be thirsty" (verse 35).

* * * * * * *

"I AM the Bread of Life." Here we see the Divine breaking in upon humanity, Jesus using the title "I AM" in His own right – the title by which God had revealed Himself to Moses. (1)

Bread here in the West is a staple food, but God has also given us life in another dimension – Spiritual life, which also needs sustenance. Here too, we see Jesus beginning to unveil the purpose behind His Death. (2) As a result our spirits, moribund through rebellion against our Creator, can receive the Spiritual resources – His Body and Blood – and, liberated by His Death, be resuscitated and restored.

What anguish we, like the Jews, cause Jesus, drawing back after the thrill of encounter with Him and being filled with His Spiritual Food. We find the change of step in the Dance too demanding, we misunderstand the nature of His Kingdom, dislike and place strictures on His Words. What He says threatens our traditional views. So, two thousand years later, Jesus' Kingdom remains diminished because Christians do not wish to accept what He says, but put their own interpretation on His Words, as the Jews did on His five challenging statements.

a)   (Verses 26-34) Like the Jews, neither do we see beyond the physical food, wanting proofs and signs – even instant results to our prayers. Yet we will not fully trust God Who provides our bread (for us to receive) and Who anointed and sealed Jesus as Messiah to give us the TRUE BREAD which nourishes our souls for Eternal Life – Life in the Kingdom. We say "Evermore give us this bread", (3) but we are prepared to go only so far with the life of the Spirit.

130

b)   (Verses 35-37) I AM THE BREAD OF LIFE. Jesus points out that the real hunger and thirst in our lives should be for the renewal of our spirits – Salvation – and for God's Righteousness to be established in our lives. This should happen if we truly believe in Him to supply our spiritual sustenance. Instead sin, guilt, disease, disharmony, discontent and restlessness alienate us from our Life-giving source.

c)   (Verses 38-51) Jesus' hearers could not believe that Jesus was the LIVING BREAD from HEAVEN, which is life-giving, as opposed to manna in the wilderness, with no special properties for Eternal Life. They thought they knew His origins and parents, (4) so His claim to be their Heavenly Messiah could not be validated in their eyes. Likewise today many people say they believe in God, even that Jesus was a good Man but not the Son of God. And they cannot believe that God is interested in them. Jesus, however, stressed God's total interest in us precisely because He came to earth to fill us with His Life. How badly the world and the Church need that Bread of Life amid violence, greed, hatred, fear and insecurity which all prevent us from using all our resources for the Kingdom.

d)   (Verses 52-59) "WHOEVER EATS MY FLESH AND DRINKS MY BLOOD HAS ETERNAL LIFE." Eating flesh with blood still in it was anathema to the Jews. And we, too, so often try to force Jesus' teaching into our mould rather than accept that His Body and Blood, shed for us, has healing power with Life-giving properties for our souls – whatever our understanding of His Words.

e)   (Verses 60-71) Jesus' last trump card was to argue that His RETURN in GLORY to HEAVEN, whence He came, was the seal of His pledge to release Spiritual power and Life for us.

Jesus knew that the Gospel would affront people because it enters the realm of Faith and Mystery.

Father, we thank You that You entered our world as a Human Being and that You have used signs that we can understand. Increase our faith and our spiritual awareness, so that we may never doubt You; and hasten that day when Your Glory shall be revealed.

To think through:

i.   What does Jesus mean by saying "I AM the Bread of Life"?
      (Read Exodus 3 vv 14-16.)

ii.   Do you believe in a living God Who has the power to transform
      lives? If so, what difference does it make to you?

iii. How can the "Bread" release spiritual power for us?

(1)   See Exodus 3 v 14; Isaiah 41 vv 4 and 10; 42 vv 6 and 8; 43
      vv 3, 13, 15 and 25.
(2)   See also Ephesians 1.
(3)   John 6 v 34 Authorised Version.
(4)   See also Mark 3 vv 31-35; 6 vv 1-6; Matthew 12 vv 46-50;
      13 vv 53-58; Luke 4 vv 16-30; 8 vv 19-21; John 7 vv 3,
      10 and 40-44.

4. "I AM THE TRUE VINE"

(John 15 vv 1-17.)

"I AM the true vine, and my father is the vinedresser... Abide in me and I in you... I AM the vine, you are the branches" (verses 1, 4, 5) (Revised Standard Version).

* * * * * * *

Anyone who has watched skaters dancing together on ice will know how they have learnt to work as one to achieve such high standards of perfection. All other thoughts are pruned for their performances to bear fruit. Likewise Jesus and the Father, although theirs is a mutual relationship of perfect harmony in the Spirit of Love. (1) Yet Jesus shows that even He, as the True Vine, cannot exist without His Father, the Vinedresser or Gardener. (2) Just as a vine grows by God-given sun and rain, so Jesus receives Love from the Father, which He reciprocates.

This Love bears fruit in the shedding of His Blood, to save us. (3) Those who receive Him reciprocate His Love, thus reproducing that mutual relationship between the Father and Himself, and becoming the first-fruits of His Love. But Jesus does more than just link us with God as in the sprinkling of blood in the Old Covenant. (4) He unites His followers with Himself. (5) He is now the Vine, rather than the old Israel, (6) and His disciples are the branches, the New Israel. So Spirit-filled, Life-giving sap can flow through Jesus to His disciples. We receive this life by faith and in the Eucharist, asking for forgiveness – and He is faithful and just to cleanse us. (7)

Jesus bids us, His dancers, learn to keep in harmony with Him so that we, too, may bear spiritual fruit. (8) This can happen only as we allow the Holy Spirit to act as a Divine searchlight and catalyst in our hearts, showing us those parts of our nature that need pruning or changing. Sometimes the painful experiences of life, which are not given, but allowed, by God, produce fruits of bitterness and resentment. And these need pruning to enable us to deepen our relationship with Him. However, if we neither appropriate His Love for ourselves and others, nor allow ourselves to be changed, then we stand to be cut off from God at the end of the Age. (9) Indeed, apart from Him we shall have nothing but troubles and sorrows.

Yet those disciples who abide in Christ by communicating with Him will know a sense of harmony, well-being and joy, despite sorrows. Whatever we ask in accordance with His Name (10) or Personality and Purpose, will be granted either as yes, no or wait, as it was for the Centurion, who never doubted Jesus' authority. His servant lived. (11)

Remaining in union with Jesus is important for ourselves and for the whole Body of Christ. (12) His Church suffers if even only one member suffers, sins or is cast out, much as our bodies suffer if we break a limb, or have an amputation. Our sin and suffering must cause God to suffer, too. (12) And disunity and deviations cause the Body of Christ to be weak and ineffective in the world's eyes, unable to influence it or counter evil. We may not reach or want uniformity of worship on earth, yet it behoves us to be united with our fellow Christians by our common belief in the risen Christ and sharing of worship. This we can only do as we abide in Him. (13)

134

"The Body of Christ, like our own bodies, is composed of individual, unlike cells that are knit together to form one Body. He is the whole thing, and the joy of the Body increases as individual cells realise they can be diverse without becoming isolated outposts." (14)

To think through:

i. What happens to Christians when they try to "go it alone"? Can you share any occasions when you have "gone it alone"?

ii. Why is the comparison of our life in Christ with a vine such a good one?

iii. What happens to the Church if even one member is out of harmony?

(1) See John 5 v 20.
(2) See John 5 v 19; John 15 v 1.
(3) See Romans 5 vv 9-11; Ephesians 1 v 7.
(4) See Exodus 24 vv 4-8.
(5) See Romans 6 vv 5-10; II Corinthians 5 v 17.
(6) See Isaiah 5 vv 1-7; Psalm 80 vv 8-16.
(7) See I John 1 v 9.
(8) See Galatians 5 vv 22-23.
(9) See Matthew 3 vv 7-10; Luke 3 vv 7-9; et al.
(10) See John 14 v 13; 15 v 16; 16 vv 23 and 26.
(11) See Matthew 8 vv 5-13.
(12) See Romans 12 vv 4-8; I Corinthians 12 vv 12-30.
(13) See I John 4 vv 13-16.
(14) From *Fearfully And Wonderfully Made* page 33. Brand & Yancy (Hodder & Stoughton/Zondervan 1980).

VII   THE SHADOW OF THE CROSS

INTRODUCTION

The Feeding of the Five Thousand was a critical time for Jesus when many turned away from Him, so that He was led to ask the Apostles, "You do not want to leave too, do you?" (1) The question elicited the reply from Peter "Lord, to whom shall we go? You have the words of eternal life." (2)

This week we prepare to share in the sufferings and Death of Jesus and try to understand their meaning for us and the world in the light of Eternity.

(1)   John 6 v 67.
(2)   John 6 vv 68-69.

* * * * * * *

1.   THE MESSIAH ENTERS JERUSALEM AND THE TEMPLE
IN TRIUMPH

(Mark 11 vv 1-11 and 15-19; Matthew 21 vv 1-17; Luke 19 vv 28-46; John 12 vv 12-19 and 2 vv 13-25.)

Those who went ahead and those who followed shouted, "Hosanna! Blessed is he who comes in the name of the Lord" (Mark 11 v 9).

* * * * * * *

So often we have greeted political leaders with their manifestos, heralding the dawn of yet another Utopia, and been disappointed...

The crowds, rejoicing triumphantly at first, were later disappointed with Jesus, too, because His manifesto did not appear to include freeing them from the Romans.

What then was there triumphant for Jesus, His journey so soon afterwards ending in His sacrificial death?

a)   This journey had been planned as part of God's overall purpose. Jesus need not have gone up to the Feast openly, but unlike previously (1) He chose to do so this time with Divine calm and poise, knowing that the Hour when He should die had arrived (2). And He would already be looking beyond Death to its reversal in triumphant Resurrection.(3)

Every detail of that journey had been arranged – the unbroken colt, the passwords for the Apostles, the timing. Yes, it had been planned, too, to coincide with the very time that the Passover pilgrims were arriving chanting the Festal Pilgrim Psalms, (4) and waving branches of palm trees, as they were accustomed to do at major festivals, (5) so that all the Messianic prophecies were fulfilled but also spiritualised. Jesus' way was so different from previous triumphal entries of politico-religious "saviours" like the Maccabees. (6) Yet the crowds at that moment believed He might be their Saviour-King in their fight for national freedom, accorded Him the honours due by laying down their garments for Him (6) and, albeit coincidentally, shouted the appropriate Messianic psalms whilst waving branches.

b)   Jesus rode on an ass, symbol of love and peace, (7) thus finally quashing Jewish belief and the temptation about earthly Kingship. (8) He was publicly declaring His Reign of Love and Peace, which He had been quietly preaching throughout His Ministry (9).

c)   The journey ended with Jesus entering His Father's House in triumph, with all the dignity of Messiahship, fulfilling Malachi's prophecies. (10) He came suddenly to His Temple, (11) where He began and ended His public appearances, (11) striding through the courtyards, ousting the marketeering and trafficking, cheating and swindling merchants. So, with His cord of whips as a symbol of His Messianic authority, Jesus cleansed and purified Temple worship...

What has the Triumphal Entry to say to us?

a)   Triumph in the Kingdom can come only by careful planning in our own spiritual lives and in the life of the Church. Talking to and listening to God, meditating on His Holy Word, prayer and praise in fellowship with other Christians and evangelism are essential. Such planned strategy can let the devil and the world know that we are in business, and want to 'catch' people for the Kingdom in a calm and dignified way.

b)   The pilgrims sang "Hosanna! Blessed is he who comes in the name of the Lord!... Hosanna in the highest." (12) On entering the Temple courtyards, the pilgrims would also recite "Open for me the gates of righteousness" and the Gatekeeper would reply "This is the gate of the Lord through which the righteous may enter..." (13) We need the Saviour Messiah to help us to open the "Gates of Righteousness" – make an end of quarrelling, bitterness and jealousy, coming to our brothers in love and peace. We need also to maintain absolute standards of righteousness and morality so that God's Kingdom may indeed triumph over evil.

c)   We need to review what is happening on Sundays and Good Friday with trading creeping in and generally relaxed standards of worship and why so many people are no longer committing their lives to Christ and His worship. Perhaps the fact that some who are lonely shop on Sundays is an issue that needs addressing by the Church. And we should send the devil fleeing with our triumphant Resurrection cry "This is the Day that the Lord has made; let us rejoice and be glad in it." (14)

"Blessed is he who comes in the name of the Lord! ... Hosanna in the highest !" (12) – Save Lord.

To think through:

i.   What has the Triumphal Entry got to say to us today in the light of what it meant for Jesus?

ii.   How can we plan our lives according to God's overall purpose?

iii.   What kind of welcome do you think that we personally, and the

Christian Church as a whole, would give Jesus if He were to come now and how do you think He would feel about life today?

(1)	See John 7 vv 1-11.
(2)	See John 7 v 6; 12 vv 27-34.
(3)	See Mark 8 v 31; 9 vv 9-10 and 30-32; 10 vv 32-34.
(4)	See Psalms 113-118; known as the Hallel, the Psalms of the Journey.
(5)	See John 12 v 13. Leviticus 23 v 40 mentions palm branches for the Feast of Tabernacles.
(6)	See I Maccabees 13 v 51; II Maccabees 10 v 7 (Apocrypha) (Authorised Version).
(7)	See Zechariah 9 v 9.
(8)	See Matthew 4 vv 8-10; Luke 4 vv 5-7.
(9)	See Luke 4 vv 18-19, et al.
(10)	See Malachi 3 vv 1-3.
(11)	See Malachi 3 vv 1-3 (Revised Standard Version). See also Luke 2 vv 22-52; 21 vv 37-38, et al.
(12)	Mark 11 vv 9 and 10; see also Psalm 118 vv 19-26. ('He Who comes' is a name for the Messiah. 'Hosanna' means "Save Lord, we beseech You".)
(13)	Psalm 118 vv 19 and 20.
(14)	Psalm 118 v 26.

2.   THE ANOINTING OF JESUS THE MESSIAH; PART I

(Mark 10 vv 35-45; Matthew 20 vv 20-28; see also Luke 22 vv 24-30.)

"For even the Son of Man did not come to be served, but to serve, and to give his life as a ransom for many" (Mark 10 v 45).

* * * * * * *

Many Christians work for the Lord, yet want the power and the glory for themselves. Mothers may wish this for their sons, but we, like the Apostles, should know better. How sad for Jesus to see us, like James and John and the other Apostles, vying for position in His Kingdom, despite all His words about humility, (1) service, (2) taking up one's cross, (3)and following His example. (4). It's hard for us to understand and accept the suffering service part. Jesus accepted that James and John, and many others like them, would drink the same awful cup of sorrow and suffering as He would and courageously receive the same Baptism of martyrdom as Himself. It is that humble, suffering service which alone is the true greatness that wins one the crown of glory in the Kingdom.

It was only as Jesus set us the example, becoming a Servant and giving His life as a ransom for many, that understanding could dawn. So often we, like the Jews before us, have seen the miserable failure of Kings and rulers, and even the Church in wanting power. Rather Jesus set before us this costly way, fulfilling and fusing the most profound of Jewish thoughts, and yet far surpassing them. He was the Heavenly Son of Man (5) – representative Man or Adam (5) – of mysterious origin, (6) come to intercede for us (7) and to draw us back to God. He was also that Suffering Servant-Son prophesied by Isaiah, (8) whose words were heard across the riven sky at His Baptism, spoken by the Father as He and the Spirit confirmed and set their seal on His noble and triumphant vocation. (9) And His entire Ministry was lived in the light of this. He allowed Himself to be baptised to accept His role of identifying Himself with those He came to save as the Suffering-Servant (10) – the Son of God freeing those in bondage, (11) washing

His disciples' feet, (12) suffering humiliation, rejection, degradation, even dying to save us. (13)

And is not His Church, the Body of Christ, called upon to be His anointed Suffering Servant in each generation, to free those in bondage, to anoint and heal the broken-hearted and the sick in body, mind and spirit? And, yes, the Church does indeed go to their homes – but not as yet everywhere, to sit and work alongside the poor and lonely, the world over – else why do they cry out in their desperation? We need to be anointed with the power of the Spirit and to empathise with – come alongside the high-rise flat dweller, the homeless, or wanderer, the inner-city dweller, the glue sniffer, drug addict or prostitute each in his or her search for meaning, happiness or love. Yes, we must be aware of the needs of such – both spiritual and emotional, the deep hidden fears underlying these situations, and bring them the Good News of deliverance from suffering. And oft-times this will mean humiliation, degradation and rejection in the eyes of the world.

Only as the Church sets out to meet the people where they are and in its area can it hope to redeem the world. Otherwise the world will seek to provide alternative services offering so-called 'help', but not necessarily the Love of Christ.

Lord, grant that we, as members of Your Church, may really undertake the responsibility of being Your servants, anointed to suffer with and on behalf of the world.

To think through:

i.   What should be the marks of Christians anointed to be Christ's suffering servants in the world today?

ii.   How are our church and the Body of Christ called upon to be the anointed servants of Jesus and to whom shall we go?

iii. What will those whom Jesus 'sends' aim to do and achieve?

(1)   See Luke 14 vv 7-11.
(2)   See Mark 9 vv 33-37.
(3)   See Mark 8 vv 34-38; Matthew 10 vv 38-39; Luke 14 vv 25-27; et al.
(4)   See Mark 8 vv 31-33; 9 vv 9-13; 10 vv 32-34 and 45.
(5)   See Daniel 7 vv 9-14; Romans 5 vv 6-21 especially 12-14 and 17.
(6)   See Matthew 1 and 2; Luke 1 and 2; Mark 6 vv 1-6; Luke 3 v 21; 4 vv 21-24.
(7)   See Hebrews 6 vv 19-21; 7 v 25.
(8)   See Isaiah 42 vv 1-4; 44 vv 1-4; 52 vv 7-53 especially v 12; 61 vv 1 and 2. Pais – ΠΑΙΣ – in Greek means Servant and Son.
(9)   See Matthew 3 vv 13-17; Mark 1 vv 9-11; Luke 3 vv 21-22.
(10)   See 4 above.
(11)   See Luke 4 vv 16-30 especially vv 18-19; cf Isaiah 61 vv 1 and 2.
(12)   See John 13 vv 2-17.
(13)   See Romans 5 vv 6-21.

3.   THE ANOINTING OF JESUS THE MESSIAH: PART II

(Mark 14 vv 1-9; also in Matthew 26 vv 6-13; John 12 vv 1-8;

compare Luke 7 vv 36-38 in VI 1.)

A woman came with an alabaster jar of very expensive perfume, made of pure nard. She broke the jar and poured the perfume on his head… "She poured perfume on my body beforehand to prepare for my burial" (Mark 14 vv 3-8).

* * * * * * *

Ointments and perfumes were a necessity in the Palestine of Jesus' time, to refresh oneself in the heat. Such unguents were very costly. Ordinary and poor people would have had very little. We are not told whether the various women, including, as John relates, Mary, the sister of Lazarus and Martha, who anointed Jesus, were rich or poor. (1) Yet they anointed Him out of love for Him, for what He had done for them and for the sense of dignity and self-respect He had given them. (2) Jesus graciously accepted this anointing as a mark of respect and honour due to a Prophet and love and devotion to Him Who was also the Son of God. He also accepted this anointing as symbolic of His Messiahship – of being the Lord's Anointed Suffering Servant. (3) Jesus, however, realised that some of those present thought that such a jar, if sold, could keep a poor man for a year and said that the problem of the poor would still always be there when He was gone. He was, however, not being callous for He was being anointed precisely for those very people – the poor, the down-trodden and outcasts of society – that He had come to save. And he had come to serve and save by suffering, dying and rising again, as their Saviour. (4)

Furthermore, Jesus knew that there would be no time to anoint His Body before burial with the Passover about to start. So this woman was doing it beforehand, for by anointing His Head she was symbolically anointing His Body, too. Jesus was eternally grateful to her for such a beautiful action. Consequently this would be remembered wherever the Gospel is told for giving her most fragrant and costly offering and returning love for Love received…

Just as the Church is God's anointed Servant, so, too, are we who comprise His Body. Shall we not want to return Jesus' most wonderful and sacrificial Love by using our costliest gifts in love, and our whole lives in His service? In loving and serving Christ we are touching the lives of His family, and in loving and serving even the least and most unlovely of His children we are indeed offering Him our costliest love. We can give money in plenty till it hurts and this is important sacrificial giving, but this is only half the story. We need also to be anointed daily in the Spirit. Then we shall go out in His strength, not ours, taking the oil of gladness with us, that is, the healing touch of Christ and His Gospel of liberation from sin and bondage. And how badly we need this amid the awful, agonising, wasteful suffering of this century.

Many relief workers, doctors, nurses and carers work for, and identify themselves with, those who are made homeless, hounded out of their country and pushed into over-crowded camps through war, revolution and famine. They empathise with their misery in their loss of human comforts and dignity and in their suffering, diseases and wounds from the ravages of war. Many indignities are inflicted for the sake of political power and conflict. As God's anointed suffering servants they help to reverse bitterness as people see God's Love and care reaching out to them and we thank Him for their selfless work.

Lord, grant that we may seek to bring the oil of gladness to others, coming to them with Your peace and proclaiming Your forgiveness. Grant that we may suffer alongside those who are heart-broken, console and bring them hope, joy and light.

To think through:

i.   How can we touch the lives of those who are the poor, the outcasts or "lepers" in society?

ii. What can we do to show such love as the woman in this story? How can we be the anointed servants of Jesus?

iii. Is suffering service, (like that of those who work with the world's poorest, the starving or victims of warfare, famine and sickness at home or abroad), or sacrificial giving of money more important?

(1)   See references at head of chapter.
(2)   See Luke 8 v 2.
(3)   See Isaiah 61 vv 1 and 2; Luke 4 vv 18 and 19.
(4)   See Mark 2 v 17; 10 v 45; Luke 15; 19 vv 1-10.

4.   A   PREPARATIONS FOR THE LAST SUPPER

(Mark 14 vv 12-16; see also Matthew 26 vv 17-19; Luke 22 vv

7-13.)

The disciples left, went into the city and found things just as Jesus had told them. So they prepared the Passover (Mark 14 v 16).

* * * * * * *

Preparations for the Last Supper, as for every Passover Feast, were a very important part of the meal, taking time and effort and on this occasion in a different place. As President, Jesus was responsible for providing a room, the special Passover plates, goblets and candlesticks. The disciples were to prepare the food and meal itself. Luke, however, states that Jesus asked Peter and John to prepare this Passover meal (1). This involved fetching the water, obtaining the Passover lamb slain at the Temple, buying the special Passover food from the markets, roasting the lamb and setting the table.

It was at this meal that Jesus spoke the words over the Bread and the Wine which were to become the symbols of the world's Salvation, so that we might be present at His Wedding Feast.

What preparations then are necessary for such a joyful event that will last through Eternity? Jesus Himself has already provided the House, (2) the Feast and the Food, for He is our Food and Drink – "the Lamb that was slain from the creation of the world". (3) Our task is to prepare ourselves by following His signs. First, we accept His Love and Righteousness, allowing Him to account us as righteous. (4) Then we exchange the rags of our old life for the fine linen Wedding clothes of our righteousness in Him. (5) And to maintain our righteousness we need to take time and effort as we ask the Holy Spirit to take over our lives, (6) follow God's instructions in His Holy Word, (6) and "feed on Him (Jesus) in our hearts by faith with thanksgiving." (7)

B THE BETRAYER

(Mark 14 vv 17-21; Matthew 26 vv 20-25; Luke 22 vv 14 and 21-23;

John 13 vv 18 and 21-30; see also Psalm 41 v 9.)

Jesus said…"One of you will betray me – one who is eating with me"… "Woe to that man" (Mark 14 vv 18 and 21).

* * * * * * *

Judas Iscariot may have come from Kerioth, (8a) or perhaps he may have been one of The Sicarii, Dagger-men – who were fanatic nationalists, or Zealots, (8b) plotting against the Romans. Either way, he was a man apart from the other Apostles, who mostly came from Galilee. At the same time he was the little band's treasurer (9) but his companions have not a word to say in his favour, calling him a thief, (9) a traitor (10) and one into whose soul satan had entered. (11) Jesus, too, knew that Judas would betray Him after feeding the Five Thousand. (12). And at the Last Supper He told him to perpetrate his deed quickly. "Better for him if he had not been born." (13)

One asks, did Jesus choose Judas deliberately to bring about God's Plan for His Death? Maybe, yet in the last resort Judas was responsible for his actions and misuse of free-will. He even rejected the offer of Grace to change his mind at the Last Supper when Jesus shared the gravy-bowl with him and again when He called him "friend" in Gethsemane, in Matthew's account .

Was Judas' betrayal then the act of a wicked man who could not stand such goodness? He does indeed appear to try to force Jesus to declare Himself as their warrior-Messiah, thus arrogantly playing the part of God. Certainly he never seemed to retract till it was too late. (14)

There goes each of us but for the grace of God Who has delivered us from the dominion of darkness. (15) Yet may there not still be a little of the Judas in each of us? Are we strictly honest with our money allowances and tithing, with our income-tax returns, even our employer's goods? Who has not thought to use force against warring nations or to settle factions? Who has not tried to force God's hand, calling on Him to declare Himself and stop evil? And who of us has not at some time done something that we knew to be wrong?

Lord, grant that we may accept Your grace in repentance and joy in preparation for Your Feast.

To think through:

i.   What preparations do we need to make for the Wedding Feast? (Read Galatians 3 vv 6-8 and 5 vv 22-23 and Revelation 19 v 8.) How important is preparation or can we leave it to God's work of grace in us?

ii.   Why do you think that Jesus chose Judas as an Apostle? In what ways might there be a bit of Judas in each of us?

iii. Was Judas' betrayal the act of a wicked man who could not stand the goodness of Jesus? Was he arrogantly playing the part of God in trying to force Jesus to declare Himself as Messiah; or did he genuinely believe in what he was doing?

(1)   See Luke 22 vv 7 and 8.
(2)   See John 14 vv 1 and 2.
(3)   Revelation 13 v 8.
(4)   See Romans 6 v 9; Galatians 3 vv 6-8 and 14.
(5)   See Revelation 19 v 8.
(6)   See John 14 vv 15-17; 16 vv 7-11; II Timothy 3 v 16.
(7)   See page 180, Order I of the Holy Communion, Common Worship of the Church of England (2000).
(8)   a. Site uncertain.
      b. Simon was also a Zealot, or a Cananaean, its earlier form.
(9)   See John 12 v 6; 13 v 29.

See Mark 14 vv 10-11; John 6 vv 70-71; 13 v 27 et al.
(11)   See John 13 v 27.
(12)   See John 6 vv 70-71.
(13)   Matthew 26 v 24.
(14)   See Matthew 27 vv 3-10.
(15)   See Colossians 1 v 13.

5. JESUS, SERVANT OF ALL

(John 13 vv 3-20; see also Mark 10 v 45; Luke 22 vv 24-30.)

Jesus...rose from supper...and girded himself with a towel...and began to wash the disciples' feet... When he had washed their feet... he said to them..."If I, then, your Lord and Teacher, have washed your feet, you also ought to wash one another's feet" (verses 3, 4, 5, 12, 14) (Revised Standard Version).

* * * * * * *

It must have been a very solemn and poignant moment for the Apostles when Jesus, girded with only a towel, began to wash their feet – a smelly task reserved for the lowest servant. Although a host might occasionally perform this ceremony as a mark of honour, His disciples were surprised, especially Peter, who arrogantly asserted that he should not have his feet washed by the Man Whom he had come to believe was the Messiah. (1) Yet, since no servant was present, none of the Apostles had apparently volunteered to perform this service before the meal.

At first the disciples could only obey, as servants. Only later did the truth of Jesus' actions dawn on them. Jesus, God's Son, had taken "the very nature of a servant" and "became obedient to death- even death on a cross". (2) And in His Servant role He had symbolically washed them – the dirty part of them – and was therefore doing more than just washing their feet or even setting them an example. He was cleansing and incorporating them into His mystical Body through His Death. And He cleanses and incorporates all those who are baptised into His Death today, (3) whether by being sprinkled with, or totally immersed in water, or in a ceremony of Dedication. Jesus, the Suffering Servant-Son had come to claim His Bride, (4) the Body of faithful believers who allow themselves to be thus baptised into His Death.

Being incorporated into the Body of Christ is the most exhilarating experience of joy, our spirits being re-united with Jesus' very Spirit. Once a member we are no longer His Servants but His friends, (5)

150

and no longer alienated from Him. (6) And as we meet other members of the Body there is a mutuality and warmth of love that comes from knowing that one belongs. And from that secure position we can reach out in love to others.

Indeed the privilege of friendship with Jesus brings responsibility towards others. Moses, God's Servant, (7) was also a friend of God, (8) and he certainly had responsibilities, like those we are called upon to undertake. Like him (9) we must be leaders, messengers of the Good News pointing and taking people to Jesus. Moses was also a Law-giver and a judge, (10) and it is our task to spell out God's Holy Law of Love to those who would listen. Furthermore, Moses interceded (11) for the Israelites and so must we intercede for this world so full of anguish and sorrow, for people who encounter death on their doorsteps, whether in the Middle East or Africa, in football stadia, on land, at sea or in the air. So, too, like Moses we must be burden-bearers, (12) mourning, weeping and shouldering the burdens of those about us, and bathing their wounds and the lack of love in their lives. Above all Moses was meek (13) and faithful. (14) Like Moses (9) we need to remove our shoes, in humility to receive God as He "washes" our feet as well as bear ourselves humbly before others who need us to "wash" their feet. And are we not required to be meek and faithful like him whom Jesus saw as the prototype of Himself, Who is the Suffering Servant? (15)

Yet we need to beware that we do submit to being cleansed, which apparently Judas was inwardly unwilling to do, and which at first Peter was too proud to accept. Alas, there is still evil, even in the Body of Christ, which must be rooted out before the great Feast starts.

Lord, grant that we may submit to Your cleansing action and so become like lights in a dark world, to point people to You.

To think through:

i.   How does Baptism change us and incorporate us into the Body of Christ? (Read Romans 5 vv 1-11; 6 vv 3-10; II Corinthians 5 vv 14-15.)

ii.   What responsibilities can we see that we need to shoulder as
      members of the Body of Christ? Is this a burden or a joy?

iii. For whom are we to bear responsibility and how?

(1)   See Mark 8 vv 27-30; Matthew 16 vv 13-20; Luke 9 vv
      18-21; John 6 vv 66-69.
(2)   Philippians 2 vv 7 and 8.
(3)   See Romans 6 vv 3 and 4.
(4)   See Revelation 19 v 7.
(5)   See John 15 v 15.
(6)   See Colossians 1 v 21.
(7)   See Deuteronomy 34 v 5.
(8)   See Exodus 33 v 11.
(9)   See Exodus 3 and 4.
(10) See Exodus 18 vv 13-23; 20 et al.
(11) See Numbers 11 vv 2-25.
(12) See Exodus 17 v 4; 32 v 11.
(13) See Numbers 12 v 3.
(14) See Numbers 12 v 7; Hebrews 3 v 5.
(15) See John 3 v 14.

6.   "THIS IS MY BODY; THIS IS MY BLOOD": CRUCIFIXION

(Mark 14 vv 22-25; Matthew 26 vv 26-29; Luke 22 vv 17-20; see also

VI B 2, 3, 4; John 19 vv 18 and 34-35; I Corinthians 11 vv 23-26.)

While they were eating, Jesus took bread, gave thanks and broke it, and gave it to his disciples, saying, "Take it; this is my body". Then He took the cup, gave thanks and offered it to them… "This is my blood of the (new) covenant, which is poured out for many (for the forgiveness of sins)" (Matthew 26 v 28, Mark 14 vv 22-24; see also the other references).

* * * * * * *

The curtain rises on the final stages in the dénouement of the drama in which a loving God wrought our Salvation through the Last Supper-Crucifixion events. The most sacred "Hour" (1) in history dawned when Jesus declared the Bread and Wine were His Very Body and Blood through the mystery of His Death. (2) They were the seals by which He established His Kingdom, the Old Covenant giving way to the NEW Covenant.

What then, precisely, was Jesus doing for us in offering us the Bread and Wine as His Body and Blood?

As ***Creator***, Jesus ***TOOK*** the disciples' offerings of Bread and Wine, and He takes ours, to consecrate them for our use. Through the Bread, a staple food which was used without leaven, or yeast, for the Passover, (3) and the Wine Jesus was doing something new. In that simple action He took the lives of the Apostles, and He takes our lives, our money, our efforts and our toil. He takes all that is good and bad in our sullied lives to transform and heal us at the deepest levels of our being.

As ***President*** of the meal Jesus gave the ***BLESSING and THANKSGIVING*** for physical nourishment over the Bread and Wine which He offered to the Father. So, too, our offerings are lifted up for Blessing and Thanksgiving for the abundant Spiritual power to be received for our use in response to the offering.

As ***both Priest and Victim*** Jesus ***BROKE*** the Bread and ***POURED OUT*** the Wine. And in a mystery Jesus declared that the Bread and the Wine were His Body and Blood. His Body was broken on the Cross by the piercing of the nails and His Blood poured forth at the thrust of the sword. That Body was broken and that Blood was shed forth in sacrifice for the world, its sin and agonising, wasteful suffering and to restore all people to Life in Him. (4) There hung our Saviour, broken, torn and bleeding so that all mankind might find Salvation and feed on Him. The action was timeless and unrepeatable. (5) And whenever the Eucharist is celebrated, that offering and sacrifice for all people, everywhere, is recalled and remembered. And Jesus, Our Saviour still cries out to all who would receive Him: "This is my body" broken for you; "This is my blood ...which is poured out for many"…(6) and for Mary, and for John. Immeasurable Love… We are baptised into His sufferings and Death, buried mysteriously with Him and raised to Eternal Life, (7) like the seed which 'dies' only to burst forth later, burgeoning with new life. (8)

As ***Host*** Jesus ***GIVES BACK*** to His followers the very Bread and Wine offered to the Father. And the faithful receive new life, blessing, forgiveness and healing through the transforming work started when the Bread and Wine were taken and sealed with Spirit-charged power.

So we receive His Life-giving Body and Blood and we are changed. And the Body and Blood are also for sharing, to show our union with

154

Jesus and our fellowship with each other in the Community of the Body.

Inasmuch as we also reach out and touch others, the world is changed, albeit slowly.

"May we who share Christ's body live his risen life; we who drink his cup bring life to others." (9)

To think through:

i.   What do the words, "This is My Body" and "This is My Blood" mean for each one of us?

ii.   How do "The Body and Blood" of Jesus make a difference to us?

iii.   Jesus' Death was for all people everywhere. How can we make this a reality in our own age?

(1)   See John 13 v 1; 17 v 1.
(2)   See Mark 14 vv 22 and 24 et al.
(3)   See Exodus 12 v 15 et al; I Corinthians 5 vv 6-8.
(4)   See Romans 5 vv 12-21.
(5)   See Hebrews 9 v 28; 10 v 10; I Peter 3 v 18.
(6)   Mark 14 vv 22-24.
(7)   See Romans 6 vv 1-11; II Corinthians 5 v 17; Colossians 2 v 12; 3 vv 1-4.
(8)   See John 12 v 24.
(9)   Page 182 in the Holy Communion service of "Common Worship" of the Church of England (2000).

7. THE BURIAL: THE PARABLE OF THE VINEYARD, AND JESUS IN THE TOMB

A   THE PARABLE OF THE VINEYARD

(Mark 12 vv 1-12; Matthew 21 vv 33-46; Luke 20 vv 9-19.)

B   BURIAL

(Mark 15 vv 42-47; Matthew 27 vv 57-61; Luke 23 vv 50-56; John

19 vv 38-42; Acts 13 v 29.)

"This is the heir", they said, "Let's kill him" (Luke 20 v 14). Joseph took the body...and placed it in his own new tomb (Matthew 27 vv 59-60).

* * * * * * *

Jesus told a parable which still speaks to us today as clearly as it did to the Jews, and we like it no better.... God has sent many prophets throughout the ages who have been killed, first by the Jews, (1) then by Christians in "religious wars". The Jews finally put God's Son and Heir to death, rejecting the Corner- or Cap-Stone already foreseen in Psalm 118 v 22. We likewise reject that Corner-Stone and crucify Him afresh daily in every wrong and dastardly action, to our peril, whether by men of evil intent or Christians. And there will be a handing over of the Kingdom to others, just as Jesus said the Jews would find that their kingdom would be handed over to believers in the New Israel, both Jewish and Gentile.

This parable of the Vineyard fits in very well with the Burial of Jesus. Just as the tenants in the parable thought that the son and heir was dead or out of their lives, so the Jews thought that Jesus was dead and buried, out of their lives for ever when He was in the tomb. And how often we think this as we try to push God to the background in our lives, acting in pride on our own. Yet God was very much alive and acting. As Jesus died and rested in the tomb His words came to pass: the Veil of the Temple was rent and the old Jewish Religion died. (2) Its leaders were already spiritually dead…so, too, are we (and our religion) in an unredeemed state. (3) God had nevertheless planned everything.

Jesus was laid in a new tomb (4) on the eve of the Passover and symbolically there was a new beginning for the New Israel. From the moment of His Death and Burial anyone who accepts Jesus as Saviour 'dies' and is 'buried' with Him, in a mystery. Our old nature, the old Adam, is 'baptised into his death', crucified with Him so that our sinful body might be destroyed. Yet, if anyone dies and is buried with Christ, that person will also live in Christ. (5) In Baptism we are ritually cleansed and given a glorious new beginning.

However, during those twenty-four hours or so that Jesus was in the tomb He was doing more than just resting. There was intense activity. There He was, the Son of God, Lord of the Dance and the Anointed One – the Messiah, the (apparent) victim of hatred and spite. Indeed He had taken into Himself and was absorbing all the hatred and spite that mankind had ever or will ever spew out, thus triumphing over it, by swallowing destruction and death in victory. It would seem that Peter learned from Jesus that during these hours He visited and preached to all those who had died before His time, (6) to give them the same chance as us of repentance, of having their old sinful natures changed and rising in a new spiritual life.

The time spent in the tomb was important so that the Jews who might try to say otherwise (7) would know that He was indeed dead, if ever they should doubt even after the sword pierced Him.(8)

Above all during this time Jesus assumed His Resurrection Body. His human work was complete and He could fully resume the Divine Glory that He had temporarily laid aside. Yet, just as He was still Divine whilst on earth, so He was to keep His Manhood, but in a spiritual way. Indeed a glimpse of that status of His full glory was granted to Peter, James and John at the Transfiguration… And here in the two natures of Jesus is the foreshadowing of our own resurrection bodies, (9) for being made in the image of God we are to become fellow-heirs with Christ. (10)

Lord, grant that we may abide patiently in You, and be buried with You, so that You may bring forth fruit in us in Your own time.

To think through:

i.   Why was it important that Jesus was in the tomb?

ii.   What was the significance of the new tomb?

iii. Is there any likelihood that the Kingdom could be handed over to other tenants today? If so, to whom and why?

(1)   See II Kings 21 vv 1-16.
(2)   See Matthew 27 v 51; Mark 15 v 38; Luke 23 v 45; Ephesians 2 v 14; Hebrews 9 vv 8-28.
(3)   See Matthew 23 vv 27-28; Ephesians 2 v 1; Colossians 2 v 13.
(4)   See Matthew 27 v 60; Luke 23 v 53; John 19 v 41.
(5)   See Romans 6 vv 3-11.
(6)   See I Peter 3 v 19; 4 v 6.
(7)   See Matthew 27 vv 62-66; cf John 19 v 34-35.
(8)   See John 19 v 34.
(9)   See I Corinthians 15 vv 35-57.
(10)   See Romans 8 vv 13-17.

VIII

A   RESURRECTION: HALLELUJAH!

INTRODUCTION

We have watched Jesus throughout His Ministry, utterly dedicated to His mission of redeeming the world – setting people free from spiritual bondage. His Ministry was undergirded with Spiritual strength born of His relationship with His Father as His Baptism and Transfiguration* testify. And we can be glad that Jesus laid aside all other forms of Messiahship and lived a life of suffering service in obedience to His Father's desire, which brought Him to the other side of the grave and thus procured our redemption.

*I am aware that some people view the Transfiguration as a post-Resurrection experience.

* * * * * * *

1.   "HAIL THE RESURRECTION THOU!" (1)

(Matthew 28 vv 1-15; Mark 16 vv 1-11; Luke 24 vv 1-12; John 20 vv

1-18.)

The angel said to the woman, "Do not be afraid, for I know that you are looking for Jesus, who was crucified. He is not here; he has risen, just as he said" (Matthew 28 v 5)… "We know that since Christ was raised from the dead he cannot die again; death no longer has mastery over him." (Romans 6 v 9).

* * * * * * *

It seemed like a fairy tale. He had 'died', yet there he was before my very eyes – alive and talking with me. His heart had stopped beating for several minutes but the ambulance men had resuscitated him with the very latest equipment. Incredible, you say? No, it happened to a friend of mine.

Yet, if we find this true story so amazing, even by modern standards, how would we have felt that morning when tales started circulating in Jerusalem that Jesus, Whom the disciples knew lay dead in a sealed tomb, (2) was alive? And no modern equipment! No wonder they felt a mixture of joy and disbelief. (3) And then He kept appearing and disappearing, much to their consternation and was not always immediately recognisable either, as Mary Magdalene discovered. (4) Nevertheless it was true. The Author of Life was indeed alive, (5) risen from the dead as He had promised. (6) The Resurrection of Jesus is the linchpin of our faith. Without it His crucifixion would have been in vain. Paul preached Christ crucified, yes, but for him the rich content of the Good News was Christ risen from the dead. The Gospels for the most part recount the story of the Man Jesus, Whom the disciples came to recognise as the Son of God in His Crucifixion and Resurrection. Paul assumes the facts of Jesus' life and passes from those details to the meaning of the Crucifixion-Resurrection complex. His message is therefore, no less real, no less rich, and we must be thankful that the Holy Spirit could penetrate so deeply into Paul – even if sometimes one does get lost in following the thrust of his argument! For us, as for Paul, it is the risen Jesus Who makes sense of life. "It was not his birth but his death, and above all his resurrection that had actually ushered in the new day." (7)

Paul is very careful to stress that Jesus was raised from the dead by God. This would discountenance any lies about His Body being stolen (8) or that He did not die but only fainted. Yes, for Paul Resurrection was a piercing of the old order of death, physical and spiritual, and a bursting forth into a new and glorious life. It was a " 'breakthrough' of the Eternal Order into this world of sin and death, an eschatological act of God, as new as the primal act of creation." (9) It was the inauguration of the New Covenant and "involving not only a new mode of life for Christ, but also the promise of life for all who were his, and assuring them that the Power which took Christ out of the grave was available for them not merely at the end of their earthly journey but here and now." (10)

And that Power is available for us today. Christ is as alive now as He was then. He reigns today as He did then. He is still Lord. How good it is when Christians sense themselves to be the fellowship of Resurrection believers and let the joy of the Resurrection fill them and flow out from them. And where better to begin than in the Eucharistic Feast? After all, did not Jesus say at the Last Supper "Do this in remembrance of me"? (11) not just as a pious memorial of His death, but actually re-calling the fact of the Crucifixion and Resurrection into our very midst, in our own day and age. His Presence is still with us. We call to mind that He died and rose for us so that He might transform us. The seed that dies from the bloom of a beautiful flower comes forth from the ground at the right moment to produce an equally beautiful flower. And this is precisely what happens to us through Jesus. He transforms us so that what was "sown in dishonour... is raised in glory"... "it is raised a spiritual body". (12) So "if anyone is in Christ, he is a new creation; the old has gone, the new has come." (13) Our life is "hidden with Christ in God", (14) and, just as there was a mighty rending of the sealed tomb at Jesus' Resurrection, so mighty power will explode in us as we allow ourselves to be baptised into His Death and Resurrection. (15)

Already on that first Easter Day Jesus was pointing to this new order. Henceforth His relationship with His disciples was to be different. He was still the same Jesus with the same recognisable physical characteristics (even to the holes in His hands and feet and the spear marks). (16) He could still eat with them (17). Yet He was utterly transparent. He had slipped from death to Life and in doing so He had resumed His former status and Glory, soon to be crowned by His assuming His place with the Father once more in order that He could establish His Kingdom.

Love's redeeming work is done;

Fought the fight, the battle won:

Lo, our Sun's eclipse is o'er!

Lo, he sets in blood no more!

Vain the stone, the watch, the seal,

Christ has burst the gates of hell;

Death in vain forbids his rise;

Christ has opened Paradise.

Lives again our glorious King:

Where, O Death, is now thy sting?

Dying once, he all doth save:

Where thy victory, O grave?

Soar we now where Christ has led,

Following our exalted Head;

Made like him, like him we rise;

Ours the cross, the grave, the skies.

Hail the Lord of earth and heaven!

Praise to thee by both be given:

Thee we greet triumphant now;

HAIL, THE RESURRECTION THOU! (1)

162

To think through:

i.   Do you find belief in the Resurrection tenable? (Be honest. Discuss any doubts or questions you may have.) What difference does the Resurrection of Jesus make to each of us?

ii.   What does it mean to be a "Fellowship of Resurrection Believers"? Are we such in our church?

iii. How can we make the Resurrection a vital experience in our own lives, especially when the going is hard?

(1)   See "Love's Redeeming Work is Done" (C. Wesley. English Hymnal 135).
(2)   See Matthew 27 vv 60-66; Mark 15 v 46; Luke 24 v 2; John 20 v 1.
(3)   See Matthew 28 v 8; Mark 16 v 8; John 20 v 20; Luke 24 vv 5, 11, 25, 37, 41.
(4)   See John 20 vv 11-18.
(5)   See Acts 3 v 15.
(6)   See Matthew 28 v 6; Mark 16 v 7; Luke 24 v 6.
(7)   *From First Adam to last*. C.K. Barrett page 91 (A & C Black 1962).
(8)   See (2) above.
(9)   *The Gospel According to St Paul* page 112. A.M. Hunter (SCM 1966).
(10) Ibid.
(11) See VII 6.
(12) I Corinthians 15 vv 42-44.
(13) II Corinthians 5 v 17.
(14) Colossians 3 v 3.
(15) See Romans 6 vv 3 and 4.
(16) See John 20 vv 27 and 28.
(17) See John 21 vv 1-14.

2. JESUS MAKES HIMSELF KNOWN IN THE BREAKING OF

BREAD AT EMMAUS

(Luke 24 vv 13-35; see Mark 16 vv 12-13.)

When he was at table with them, he took the bread, gave thanks, broke it and began to give it to them. Then their eyes were opened and they recognised him, and he disappeared from their sight (verses 30- 31).

* * * * * * *

He lay in bed. Fear, dismay and hopelessness raged within him as he realised the extent of his losses – his family killed in that accident and he, minus a limb; and perhaps now without a job. Yet he had believed that the new life that he had begun as a minister in the Church was of God. Where was God now? Suddenly he was aware of a Presence. He could not be exactly certain at first but then, yes, there was an unaccounted bright light – and a Voice saying that He was going to honour that life he had begun in Him. Despite his losses he would know power – power from on high which would be released into his life so that he might bring many into the Kingdom...So began a new life for this once devastated servant of God.

The death of Jesus had seemed so final and Cleopas and his wife, or fellow traveller, just could not grasp it. In their grief they had apparently buried their hopes with Jesus in the tomb. "We had hoped that he was the one who was going to redeem Israel." (1) And were they still thinking of Jesus freeing them from the Romans? They could not even begin to believe the stories of the women, not even when Jesus first explained the Scriptures to them.

So often we are like these two. We wonder how Jesus can be alive and caring about us. There is so much evil in the world. We hope He might step in, but He doesn't. That would be to abrogate the free will He has given us. So all this talk of Jesus being alive today is reduced to idle speculation by many!... Someone dies, someone very close to us. Or there is the death of a hope, something that should have turned out well, but did not. Maybe we feel rejected. We grieve, and rightly so, but alas, some of us continue mourning with rage and burying our hopes instead of using such occasions to deepen our faith and trust in Him. Many do trust Him but I wonder, do we think more of our own plans and the way we would have done something rather than waiting on God and seeking how He would do it; do we turn misfortune or evil into blessing? And some of us would rather wallow self-indulgently in our misery than accept God's Sovereignty and the fact that Jesus is very much alive today. Nor do we seem to search the Scriptures with spiritual eyes or understanding. Yet, He is there, right by our side, if only we knew and used our eyes of faith! Nevertheless, notice how gentle Jesus was with the couple. First, He gave them the opportunity to grieve and share what was on their hearts. Then He gave them time to acclimatise, carefully explaining the necessity of His Death and Resurrection from the Scriptures they knew but did not understand. Yet, when they thought about it afterwards, it all made sense. Furthermore Jesus was so gracious. He waited for an invitation to stay with them rather than press Himself upon them. So the ground was prepared. And in the Breaking of Bread they KNEW the Risen Lord…

So, too, Jesus gently leads us through our doubts and griefs. He knows how difficult it is for us to grasp that He is alive. Our hopes seem to lie buried. Yet He gives us many pointers along the way. Re-birth occurs yearly in nature. The Scriptures plainly reiterate the Resurrection events. And we meet with those who have in some way encountered the Risen Lord spiritually and been changed by the experience. Sometimes we may feel uncomfortable. They are so sure and so joyful. Yes, indeed, He is there, in a friend, or their actions, in the Scriptures or Breaking of Bread, as we share round the table, foreshadowing that Eternal Feast when every eye shall behold Him. (2)

Lord, how graciously You showed Yourself to Your two disciples on the road to Emmaus. How patiently You waited as they poured out their grief. How gently You accepted their delay in recognising You. And we know that You are the same to us today. Lord, we thank You for Your gracious patience and Love amidst our doubts, our fears and griefs.

To think through:

i.   Why do you think that God does not appear to step in to bring about an end to evil in the world? Are there any signs that He has acted and still does act or intervene?

ii.   How would you answer anyone who said that the Resurrection is idle speculation or that God does not care when He apparently allows evil to cause "good" people to suffer?

iii.   How can we turn doubt, fear and worry into faith? What signs and aids does God give us in the Bible in this day and age to help us?

(1)   Luke 24 v 21.
(2)   See Revelation 1 v 7; 22 v 4.

3. JESUS MEETS THE APOSTLES IN THE UPPER ROOM

(Luke 24 vv 36-49. See also Mark 16 vv 14-18; John 20 vv 19-23.)

Jesus himself stood among them… (And) He said to them, "Why are you troubled and why do doubts arise in your minds? Look at my hands and my feet…a ghost does not have flesh and bones as you see I have… Do you have anything here to eat?" (verses 36…42).

* * * * * * *

It was Easter evening. Can we feel the fear of the disciples, badly shaken by the trials and Crucifixion and then their own disloyalty? They had indeed gathered but locked the doors for fear of the Jews. Yet Jesus 'came' and stood in their midst. He knew that they would all be together discussing the events of the day. They were almost too scared to believe the joyful News, so He had to gently unlock the doors of their hearts and minds. He invited them to see and feel His scars and handle Him, and He asked to eat with them to prove that He was the same Jesus Who ate the Last Supper with them. He also explained that His Death and Resurrection was the only way God could demonstrate His Love for His people, costly as it was. Wickedness and death were absorbed into Himself and swallowed up in His victory over the grave. (1) Jesus thus opened the way for them to release their fears and doubts and for their shattered spirits and emotions to be restored. (2)

The result was like the release of dynamite. They were able to accept their original call (3) joyfully and their renewed commission to preach the Good News of repentance and forgiveness throughout Jerusalem and to all men everywhere (4) – not in their own strength but in the power of the Spirit, soon to come on them. (4)

Encounter and reality go hand in hand. The disciples' experience of the Resurrection was "rock" solid. (5) The tomb was indeed empty, (6) and Jesus was with them for real. (7) No-one in doubt or building on a false premise could preach with such joyful certainty that the same Jesus Christ who was crucified is indeed risen.(8) And they were witnesses of these facts. (9) He is both "LORD and CHRIST";(10) truly GOD and truly MAN in His Incarnation (though He had voluntarily limited His Divinity during His life); (11) truly GOD and truly MAN in His Resurrection, His physical Body remaining intact, which is a Divine mystery.

Twenty centuries later people are still encountering Jesus and discovering the reality of the Resurrection. All over the world Jesus is still a present reality, coming to individuals and groups, disturbing (12) the authorities who see in Him a Power greater than their own and therefore they often reject Him. Yes, encounter with Jesus is dynamite. If you think that He could not possibly unlock the doors of your heart, mind and spirit and release you from your fears and doubts, your denials, sin, suffering or illness then look and hear again. Let Jesus' encounter with this young drug addict whose nick-name was 'Jesus' and gang leader from the former Walled City of Hong Kong, have the last word.

" 'Jesus' and I sat in a café while I opened my big Bible and told him about my Jesus… He understood what I was saying… It was almost as if the Holy Spirit had come down over our formica table. 'Jesus' sat there with tears streaming down his cheeks quite oblivious of his surroundings or the pretty waitress. He prayed, asking Jesus into his life and was baptised in the Spirit in the midst of our coffee cups." (13) (In a shared meal – a sacrament in itself – much as Jesus often had with His disciples, there indeed was Jesus revealing Himself to a "tough". As new power entered his life, so it can in yours and mine as we feed on Him by faith.)

Yet such blessing is never for ourselves alone. We, too, are called to go out in the power of the Spirit to give light and life to the world.

Lord, we greet You with Joy in Your Resurrection.
And we ask You to dispel any doubts or fears that we may have.
Grant that we may put our hands in Yours, in faith,
And allow Your presence to show us the reality of Your Risen Life.

168

To think through:

i. Why do you think that the disciples missed all that Jesus had said
    about His Death and Resurrection? Is it possible that we, too, can
    miss what Jesus says to us? If so, how can we avoid this?

ii. How can we help people to have a real encounter with the Risen
    Lord?

iii. Do you know of people whose lives have been changed by such
    an encounter? If so, what difference has it made to them?

(1) See I Corinthians 15 vv 54-57.
(2) See also Mark 16 vv 8 and 14; Matthew 28 vv 4 and 8; Luke
     24 v 4.
(3) See Mark 1 vv 16-20; Mark 3 vv 13-19 et al; Luke 5 vv
     1-11.
(4) See Matthew 28 vv 16-20; Luke 24 vv 45-49; John 21 vv
     16-25; Acts 1 v 8; Acts 2f.
(5) See I Corinthians 10 vv 1-5.
(6) See Matthew 28 vv 1-6; Mark 16 vv 1-8; Luke 24 vv 1-9;
     John 20 vv 1-8.
(7) See also Acts 1 vv 1-11 et al.
(8) See Romans 1 vv 1-6; 6 vv 1-11.
(9) See Acts 2 v 32; 3 v 15; I John 1 vv 1-4.
(10) Acts 2 v 36.
(11) See Philippians 2 vv 1-11.
(12) See Acts 16 vv 35-40; Acts 17 vv 1-9; so, too, today!
(13) From _Chasing the Dragon_ page 137. Jackie Pullinger and
     Andrew Quicke (Hodder & Stoughton 1980).

4.   BREAKFAST ON THE SEASHORE

(John 21.)

Just as day was breaking, Jesus stood on the beach; ... That disciple whom Jesus loved said to Peter, "It is the Lord"... When they got out on land, they saw a charcoal fire there, with fish lying on it, and bread. Jesus said to them... "Come and have breakfast."... When they had finished breakfast, Jesus said to Simon Peter... "Do you love me more than these?" (verses 4, 7, 9, 15) (Revised Standard Version).

* * * * * * *

"Breakfast by the lakeside in the summer dawn, with fish and bread cooking on the stones." (1)

The fishermen amongst the Apostles had gone fishing whilst, it would seem, waiting for Jesus to meet them in Galilee. At first light they would scarcely recognise Who it was calling to them from the shore, yet John recognised the familiar voice and command of Jesus. (2) Their obedience led to an unusually large haul of fish, without breaking the nets. Breakfast with and cooked by the Lord followed; a poignant meal and later a conversation centering round Peter.

Galilee, suitably bordering Gentile territory, was where the Messiah was expected to inaugurate the new era of His universal Reign, and which Jesus did, in His own intrinsic way. The extraordinary catch of fish of every type was symbolic of the vast numbers of people who would come into the Kingdom from every nation. (3) And the nets speak of the perfect wholeness of the kingdom. The atmosphere in this Encounter was one of expectancy, of awe and wonder and of worship in the presence of their Risen Lord, The Lord of the Dance. The breakfast fellowship meal was a foreshadowing of that Eternal fellowship of the Wedding Feast. (4)

We can for ever be grateful that Jesus' conversation with Peter has been recorded. Peter, although obviously repentant and forgiven, (5) needed to be publicly reinstated amongst the Apostles after his denials. (6) Already he had a special role, (7) yet Jesus needed him to declare publicly whether his love could stand the test. Peter carefully avoided using a word suggesting the kind of love that involved sacrifice since he had not managed to be prepared to die with Jesus at His Trials. Now that he was completely broken he could be re-made, trusting and relying on strength from Jesus – even for the manner of his death. This Peter could then be endowed with the authority of 'team leader' for the care of souls coming into the Kingdom. Poignant, yes, and painful, yet Jesus knew He had to draw out any remains of remorse and shame which could have ruined his leadership role, over against John's long life of quiet witness. (Tradition has it that Peter was crucified upside down for Jesus later).

The post-Resurrection era saw the dawn of the age to come, the consummation of which is in God's hands. (8) However much we would like to know, or people may try to date it, that is not for us. If He seems to delay, then all we can do is to get on with our work, guided by His Spirit in us, seeking out, feeding and nurturing His sheep and lambs. For where hearts are reborn in Him, there indeed is the dawning of the Kingdom.

Jesus has all the Spiritual resources we need. They are all laid out in this Encounter. There is fellowship with Him in the Breaking of Bread, cleansing, forgiveness and healing. Only as we allow God to free us from the bondage of our denials, our sin and self-sufficiency, can we receive that deep cleansing and forgiveness which leaves no bitterness or remorse. Then we receive, or receive anew the status of 'apostle' sent out to work for the Lord as leaders, evangelists and teachers in the Kingdom. (9)

So we wait with bated breath the consummation of the Age when Jesus will appear for the Feast. (10)

Lord, we ask You to reveal Yourself to us,
To be with us as we have fellowship with You and one another.
Fill us with Your Spirit and cleanse us from our secret faults,
So that, renewed in Your love, we may go out to tend Your flock.

To think through:

i. What signs are there for us that as Jesus' disciples we are living in the dawning Age of the Kingdom?

ii. What spiritual resources are there in this event that are also there for us today?

iii. Would we be prepared to die for Jesus, or would we, like Peter at Jesus' Trials, flinch?

(1) From *Man's Concern with Holiness* page 37. A.M. Allchin. Edited by Marina Chavchavadze (Hodder & 1970).
(2) See Luke 5 vv 1-11.
(3) See also Ezekiel 47 v 10.
(4) See Revelation 19 v 9.
(5) See Luke 24 v 34.
(6) See Mark 14 vv 53-72; Matthew 26 vv 69-75; Luke 22 v 54-62; John 18 vv 15-18 and 25-27.
(7) See Matthew 16 vv 13-20; Mark 8 vv 27-29; Luke 9 vv 18-20; John 1 vv 40-42.
(8) See Mark 13 vv 32-37; Matthew 24 vv 36-44; see also Luke 17 vv 20-37; Acts 1 vv 6 and 7.
(9) See Ephesians 4 vv 11-12.
(10) See Revelation 19 v 9; 21 vv 1-5.

B   THE AGE OF THE SPIRIT

1.   ASCENSION

(Luke 24 vv 50-53; Matthew 28 vv 16-20; Mark 16 vv 19-20; see

also Acts 1 vv 6-11.)

When he had led them out to the vicinity of Bethany, he lifted up his hands and blessed them. While he was blessing them, he left them and was taken up to heaven.... and (they) returned to Jerusalem with great joy. And they stayed continually at the temple, praising God (verses 50-53).

* * * * * * *

It was the eve of Ascension. I stood tip-toe on the edge of the cliff watching the last rays of the setting sun, and the world was transfigured as the sun splayed off into golden rays. As the sun sank deeper and deeper those rays turned first orange, then crimson. I stayed, watching while the crimson rays spread over the sky and lit up the feathery wisps of cloud, tinged at the edges with plush pink and gold. And my thoughts turned to the stained glass windows in the Roman Catholic Cathedral of Christ the King in Liverpool – a Cathedral built as a crown – the crown of the Ascended Christ.

Much about Jesus' Ascension must remain a mystery. It seems, from the Gospel stories, that He appeared and disappeared many times after the Resurrection: in the Breaking of Bread; in the Upper Room; by the sea of Galilee; even perhaps transfigured on a mountain at that time as some believe. (1) Sometimes He was taken up from them; and also after what is so often regarded as the last official time that He was with His Disciples (2) He would appear, – as He did to Paul and to five hundred brethren. (2) Indeed, He has appeared to people in visions throughout the ages and He still does.

In what sense then can the stories of His Ascension be considered to be a "final" appearance? There had to be a time when the disciples said 'Goodbye' to the earthly Jesus Who had finished His work on earth. There had to be a time when Jesus, now raised from the dead, resumed His place with the Father so that the Holy Spirit could be liberated into the lives of each of us. Thus we could know the Presence of the Lord even more closely than when He walked on the earth. There had, too, to be a time when there was an acknowledgement in Heaven and on earth that Jesus was established as the King of the Kingdom. So the Ascension is seen as the day when Jesus returned to Heaven to take up His position as King. Like Kings in the Old Testament, (3) like the monarch here in Britain, He was crowned – with glory. It was Jesus' Coronation Day – a day of 'Goodbye' in one sense, but a day of blessing and when, from then on, He could be with His people everywhere and hence still able to appear as He does on every occasion when the Bread is broken. Indeed, I like to think there may have been breaking of Bread when He was parted from them.

At an earthly Coronation the King or Queen has a crown placed on his or her head and is given an orb and a sceptre, signifying power over people and the justice by which the monarch should rule.(3) This earthly Coronation, though different, can help us to understand Jesus' Ascension and Coronation better. Often in stained glass windows He is depicted wearing a halo or crown, holding a staff or sceptre and an orb, and seated in Glory above the world and reigning in triumph. Earthly Kings and Queens, being human, are still prone to sin and have no power to save us from evil and sin but Jesus is perfect and has perfected all things. For He had conquered sin and death on the Cross in that moment when He cried out "It is finished." (4) All is fulfilled. Satan and all his evil powers were vanquished and can be vanquished in each of us, even though evil still has to run its course. Back in Heaven He was given the place of honour and acknowledged as King over all. (5) His Reign of justice and peace was begun.

Justice and peace in this war-torn, famine-stricken world there may not be yet, but Jesus has won the victory and His Reign of justice and peace begins in our hearts. He has already raised our human nature above all the troubles and trials of this life – and the gift of such transformation is ours for the asking. So we say "Amen. Come Lord Jesus." (6) Come Holy Spirit.

Lord, what a dramatic moment in the lives of the Disciples when You went back to heaven, ascending on the clouds of Glory. Help us to realise that this crowning moment of Your life was when You resumed Your place in Heaven as God the Son and Man, both in their fulness. Thank you that such an event liberated You to be free to intercede for us and through Your Holy Spirit to be present with each one of us.

To think through:

i.   What is the point and significance of the Ascension?

ii.   How can the Ascension of Jesus help us today?

iii.   What facts do you find difficult about the Ascension (if any)?

(1)   See Matthew 17 vv 1-13; Mark 9 vv 2-13; Luke 9 vv 28-36; see also John 12 vv 20-36.
(2)   See Acts 1 vv 9-11; I Corinthians 15 vv 5-8.
(3)   See I Samuel 10 v 1; Psalms 2 and 110.
(4)   John 19 v 30.
(5)   See Revelation 15 vv 3 and 4.
(6)   Revelation 22 v 20.

2. PENTECOSTAL OUTPOURINGS -" RIVERS OF LIVING WATER"

(John 7 vv 37-39; Acts 2 vv 1-21.)

Jesus...said in a loud voice... "Whoever believes in me, as the Scripture has said, streams of living water will flow from within him." By this he meant the Spirit (John 7 vv 37-39). They saw what seemed to be tongues of fire that separated and came to rest on each of them. All of them were filled with the Holy Spirit and began to speak in other tongues, as the Spirit enabled them (Acts 2 vv 3 and 4).

* * * * * * *

"That night as we were praying together, suddenly the Holy Spirit came just as He did on the Day of Pentecost. In Acts Chapter 2 we read that He came from Heaven like the mighty, rushing wind. And that night, as I was sitting next to my sister, I heard this mighty, rushing sound. It sounded like a small tornado in the church. I looked around and saw nothing. I turned to my sister.

'Dear, do you hear a strange noise?' I asked.

'Yes,' she replied, 'I do. But forget about the sound, and let's pray.'

She began to pray... At first one by one, and before I knew it they all began to pray at the same time. Then I heard the fire bell ringing loud and fast... When they got to the church they saw the flames, but the church wasn't burning. Instead of a natural fire, it was the fire of God. Because of this, many people received Jesus as their Savior and also the Baptism of the Holy Spirit... Heaven came down that night... As the Holy Spirit moved, people all over the church came under conviction and accepted Jesus as their own personal Savior... And when they went out, great signs followed them..." (1) A traditional church in Indonesia whose members took God at His Word and when they prayed for a release of the Holy Spirit the above account is what happened. And so the Indonesian Revival started. The Holy Spirit began working there in power, signs and wonders following.

Power, yes, that's what Whitsun or Pentecost is all about. God's Holy Spirit has always been at work and active in the world – involved in every aspect of life, from Creation onwards. And His very Breath willed us into being. Yet, even so, although individuals had, before Christ, lived very holy lives because they were open to God, something extra happened on that festival of Pentecost. The Disciples were already waiting for the 'promise' of the Holy Spirit from the Father (2) and so they were, in a way, prepared for what was to happen. And yet when the Holy Spirit came the experience was far greater and more wonderful than they could ever have imagined. They were fairly catapulted into the streets, and they glowed with the Spirit. As they spoke, people from foreign countries could understand them.

This has been the experience of Christians down the ages and of others who have been receptive of the Lord. And this is the experience of many today: traditional churchgoers, members of house churches, non-Christians, coming under the influence of the Spirit, drug-addicts, criminals and murderers. Rivers of living water are welling up in so many people's hearts. It is wonderful to see people as they pray being caught up in light and they have known and said how they had encountered the living God.

Fire and wind, light and heat. They are all symbols and signs of God's presence and activity in our midst. The signs are still the same as at the Burning Bush (3) on Mount Horeb (4) and in the Upper Room. "Jesus Christ is the same yesterday and today and forever." (5) But be sure of this, whatever signs God chooses to give, however He chooses to work, to those who ask He gives – and in power."Streams of living water", (6) will flow out through us and change us, and then, changed, we are commissioned to go out in power, as witnesses to the uttermost parts of the earth. (7)

How we need God's Holy Spirit this century, and how God is indeed pouring His Spirit out. May He pour that same Spirit on each one of us today.

Lord, be with us as we pray to You to fill us with Your Spirit. Without You our lives are dried up, withered, lifeless. With You we shall know fulness of life and power.

To think through:

i.   Why could the Holy Spirit not come in power until Jesus had ascended?

ii. What is the true purpose behind our receiving the Holy Spirit?

iii. How can we receive the Holy Spirit and do we want to receive Him?

(1) From *Like A Mighty Wind*, Mel Tari, pages 24-25 (Kingsway 1973).
(2) See Acts 1 v 8.
(3) See Exodus 3.
(4) See I Kings 19 vv 9-13.
(5) Hebrews 13 v 8.
(6) John 7 v 38.
(7) See Acts 1 v 8.

3. FINALE: " THE WEDDING FEAST"

(Revelation 19 vv 1-10; 21 vv 1-7; 22 vv 1-5 and 12-14.)

(a) "Hallelujah! For our Lord God Almighty reigns. Let us rejoice and be glad and give him glory. For the wedding of the Lamb has come and his bride has made herself ready…"

(b) Happy are those who are invited to the ***WEDDING FEAST*** of the Lamb" (Revelation 19 vv 6, 7 and 9). (1)

* * * * * * *

When God called Israel out of Egypt He called her to be holy – separate and different from other nations. (2) Over the centuries the Israelites came to understand that God wanted His people as a treasured possession and a holy people. (2) Yet all too often the picture was far removed from this truth.

Only with Jesus do we really discover the full meaning of holiness. "Holiness is about a festival of joy, a dinner party to which all the most unlikely people are invited. For holiness is about God giving his life and love to men, and men giving their life and love to one another in a movement of joy which overflows in thankfulness to God the giver…The Gospels are full of stories about meals taken together, about family celebrations with music and dancing, when someone who has been missing suddenly turns up, about breakfast by the lake-side in the summer dawn, with fish and bread cooking on the stones. The holiness of God is always what we least expected. It works itself out in flesh and blood.

We did not expect to see the flesh and blood of a man nailed to the cross, as the centre of the way that leads to this celebration of joy… But that is how it is. For joy cannot be known in this world without suffering, and suffering in this world can be the way that leads to joy." (3)

In the back streets of many of our inner cities can be found communities of people bringing the light of God to all such unlikely people in quiet unassuming ways – to name but a few – clergy, counsellors, missionaries, and those who work with street children, drug addicts, alcoholics, single parents, the abused.

"All the most unlikely people"(3) – we have come to see that they are the drug-addicts, alcoholics, the poor and marginalised, prostitutes, drop-outs and criminals. Why is this? Simply because they know their spiritual poverty. Indeed Jesus said, "Blessed are the poor in spirit." (4) They know the measure of the difference between themselves and God and they can see just how much God loves them in Jesus. (5) They are so thankful to find someone Who accepts them as they are and in their spiritual poverty they are prepared to accept His free Gift of Salvation. They can accept the Crucifixion and Resurrection and see that Holiness is about God dying for them and rising again so as to be with them to love and help them.

So we find joy wherever the Gospel is preached and accepted, from Levi, Peter, Zacchaeus and Mary Magdalene to St Francis, Mother Teresa and 'Jesus', the young drug-addict from the now abolished 'Walled City' of Hong Kong's drug community who then led his fellow gangsters to Christ (6). Today people are being set free from fear and worry, from idolatry, witchcraft and satanism, from sin and disease, all the way from Britain to Cuba, from Chile to China and from Africa to Russia. And there is joy in these Christians. In the Gospels they gave parties (7) in thanksgiving. And in our own day people give up all they have to serve The Lord in joy, as is the case with various communities, missionaries and others who work with the disabled, the drop-outs or criminals in prisons or special hospitals and in the poorest parts of the world. And many do receive Jesus. So they bring new life and hope where there was despair, acceptance and work as well as helpful solutions for their health and that of their animals, which can bring them in an income.

We cannot earn Salvation by striving to attain it on our own merits. The joy of Salvation comes through the suffering of Jesus. Yet, once we accept Salvation, we are expected to change into our wedding clothes and pursue all righteousness in joy. A wedding is the height of rapture bringing a new beginning, new hope and the joining of the happy couple in union. So the symbol of the Wedding and its

180

festivities, its abundance, the marriage itself, is a parable. (7) It speaks
of the time when all God's children will receive of that rich abundance
(and all will be given the chance to do so). It will be the New Era of
the Kingdom when Jesus the Lamb will feed His people and satisfy
every (spiritual) need. (8)

At the beginning of our journey Jesus says "Come to me all you
who are wearied and burdened, and I will give you rest" (His Eternal
Rest) (9) And at the end of our journey we hear the Spirit and His
Bride saying "Come." (10)

"For the wedding of the Lamb has come, and his bride has made
herself ready."

"Happy are those who are invited to the WEDDING FEAST of the
Lamb." (11)

"Amen. Come Lord Jesus." (12)

* * * * * * *

God And Man At Table Are Sat Down (13)

O Welcome, all ye noble saints of old,

As now before your very eyes unfold

The wonders all so long ago foretold:

God and man at table are sat down.

Who is this who spreads the victory feast?

Who is this who makes our warring cease?

Jesus, risen Saviour, Prince of Peace.

God and man at table are sat down.

Beggars, lame and harlots also here;
Repentant publicans are drawing near.
Wayward sons come home without fear.
God and man at table are sat down.

Worship in the presence of the Lord,
With joyful songs and hearts in one accord,
And let our host at table be adored.
God and man at table are sat down.

Here He give Himself to us as Bread,
Here as wine we drink the blood He shed,
Born to die, we eat and live instead,
God and man at table are sat down.

When at last this earth shall pass away,
When Jesus and his bride are one to stay,
The feast of love is just begun that day,
God and man at table are sat down.

Song and arrangement by kind permission of Robert Stamps and Jeanne Harper.

182

To think through:

i.   What does it mean to be 'poor in spirit'?

ii.   Why does Jesus so often use the symbol of a wedding? Does it
      still suggest to us what Jesus meant?

iii. Who are the undeserving and those who, according to all sense
      of justice, would have no hope of an Invitation to the Wedding
      Feast?

(1)   (a) New International Version. (b) Jerusalem Bible.
(2)   See Exodus 19 vv 5 and 6.
(3)   From *Man's Concern With Holiness*, page 37, A.M. Allchin.
       Edited by Marina Chavchavadze (Hodder & Stoughton
       1970).
(4)   Matthew 5 v 3.
(5)   See Romans 5 vv 6-11; and the Gospel stories!
(6)   see VIII A3.
(7)   See Mark 2vv 13-17; Mark 14vv 3-9; John 12vv 1-8 et al.
(8)   See Revelation 7 v 17.
(9)   Matthew 11 v 26.
(10)   Revelation 22 v 17.
(11)   Revelation 19 v 7 Jerusalem Bible.
(12)   Revelation 22 v 20.
(13)   From *Sounds of Living Water*, 67, Robert Stamps. Betty
       Pulkingham and Jeanne Harper (Hodder & Stoughton 1977).